Ple

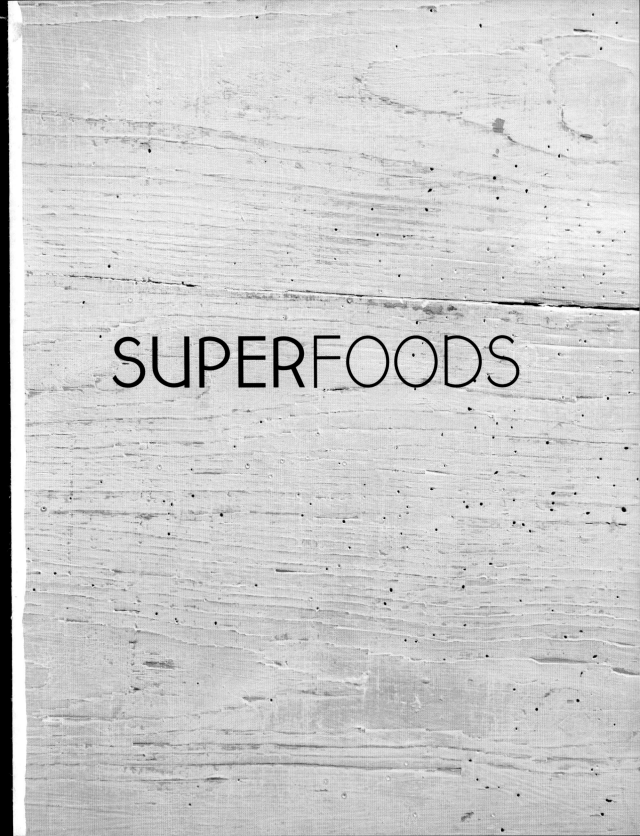

SUPERFOODS

SUPERFOODS

The flexible approach to eating more superfoods

JULIE MONTAGU
THE **FLEXI** FOODIE

Photography by Yuki Sugiura

Quadrille
PUBLISHING

Publishing Director: Jane O'Shea
Creative Director: Helen Lewis
Senior Editor: Céline Hughes
Designer: Nicola Ellis
Design Assistant: Emily Lapworth
Photographer: Yuki Sugiura
Prop Stylist: Iris Bromet
Production: Vincent Smith, Stephen Lang

First published in 2015 by
Quadrille Publishing Limited
Pentagon House
52–54 Southwark Street
London SE1 1UN
www.quadrille.co.uk

Cataloguing in Publication Data: a catalogue
record for this book is available from the
British Library.

ISBN: 978 184949 582 0

Printed in China

I've regularly compared the superfoods in this book to superheroes, and so I'd like to dedicate this book to the real superheroes in my life: my four children, Emma, Jack, William and Nestor. You are each, in your own spectacular way, a true superhero.

CONTENTS

SUPERFOODS, SUPER YOU!

There is NO diet on earth that will yield the same results for everyone. So let's throw out the word 'diet' as we have come to know it once and for all. Feel better already, right?! So, from now on let's use the proper, original definition of 'diet' when it passes through our lips. A diet is the kinds of food that a person, animal or community consistently eats. Boom, there you have it. We are not and should not be looking to ever restrict ourselves to feeling great. However, there are some basic principles of eating that we can all benefit from. In other words, yes, by being flexible you can have your cake and eat it, too. And that's why I call myself The Flexi Foodie!

THIS BOOK IS FOR EVERYONE

My 'Flexi Foodie' approach to meal times is not one of strict rules; remember we are not dieting, thank goodness! Instead, it demonstrates how it is both simple and advantageous to embrace a plant-based, superfood lifestyle – even if only on a part-time basis. I always tell my children that if they were exactly alike then life would be really boring. So, just as with my children, no two people are identical in their preferences and nutritional requirements. As a result, this book is completely inclusive – no matter what your current diet and lifestyle. Absolutely anyone and everyone can easily revolutionise their eating habits and take a giant leap down the path to long-lasting health. Instead of being an instant process, this book details how to make incremental changes to your lifestyle that serve to eradicate the bad and introduce the good.

WHERE IT WENT WRONG

But let's start at the beginning. What causes us to gain weight and what are the health issues that go hand in hand? Why are so many people getting heavier and heavier and sicker and sicker? Fortunately, studies have been examining these questions and we now finally have some answers.

Over the past 100 years our consumption of meat, dairy, sugar and processed and packaged foods have sky rocketed. That in turn has led to an increase in obesity rates and health issues. But the good news is that you can change all this very easily and I'm going to show you how!

OUT WITH THE BAD, IN WITH THE GOOD

Throughout this book and its recipes, we will focus on the foods that are most powerful for health and reduce and even eliminate the ones that aren't. But what really counts is what works for you and this is a super-easy and fun way to experiment with a new way of eating. By adding more superfoods into your diet, you will naturally start to crowd out the bad ones. I have seen so many people become slimmer, healthier and feel so much better by simply increasing the good and decreasing the bad. When people start to comment on how amazing you look, and when you start to feel better and better day by day, you'll be spurred on. For me, the extra bonus of this way of life is the abundance of energy that comes with it. You will soon notice that this translates into feeling great, every single day.

So, let's begin revolutionising your eating habits so we can get started on the journey to all the tremendous benefits. The foods that you'll want to start adding to your plate are green leafy vegetables, wholegrains, legumes, vegetables, fruits and natural sweeteners; many of these I term 'superfoods' because they're SO jam-packed with the nutrients your body thrives on. The foods that we are going to decrease and maybe eliminate completely, are animal products (this includes dairy), refined sugar, wheat and refined oils. Studies have shown that when you start to cut back on these food groups and increase your consumption of wholesome plant-based foods, your health improves – a lot!

Some people think that a plant-based diet might lack the nutrition they need when in fact the opposite is true. When you replace meat with these plant-based foods, you eliminate the animal fats and other things that can be detrimental to your health. But that's not all. You're also getting the fibre you need to keep things moving, which in turn keeps you slim. On top of that, you're keeping bad cholesterol at bay and allowing all the incredible antioxidants and vitamins to be absorbed into your cells and protect you against disease. You can also rest assured that plant-based foods are not lacking in protein. When you incorporate whole foods into your diet – dark, leafy green veg, other veggies, fruit, seeds and nuts – you will get your necessary quota of protein.

THE BOTTOM LINE:
A PLANT-BASED DIET IS NUTRIENT-RICH
– AN ANIMAL ONE IS NUTRIENT STRIPPED.

MEAT

But this book is NOT about cutting all the animal products out. It's possible to be flexible and have that piece of meat if you want to while combining it with an antioxidant, nutrient-dense side dish or pudding. But let's explore this a little bit more – in particular, oxidation, free radicals and antioxidants.

The process of oxidation within the human body damages cells. When oxygen is metabolised in the body, free radicals are created. These free radicals steal electrons from other molecules, which in turn causes damage. In today's day and age, we are being bombarded with free radicals and this overload has been linked to a whole host of diseases. Oxidation gains momentum through stress, smoking, alcohol, pollution and other factors including digestion. For example, when you eat meat it causes the digestion to work incredibly hard to breakdown the food. Simply put, it takes about twice as long to digest meat compared to plant-based foods.

Modern science believes 80 percent or more of the damage to the body is caused by free radicals. This is where the power of incorporating more plant-based superfoods into your diet becomes your superhero. Eating a range of green leafy vegetables, fruits, wholegrains, legumes and other veggies provides you with a plethora of antioxidants. Not only do these antioxidants neutralise free radicals, but they remove the free radicals from the cells which in turn will prevent or reduce the damage caused by oxidation.

DAIRY

Dairy is another one that I feel needs to be cut right back or cut right out. We are the only species on the planet that still consumes milk past the infancy stage. And, in fact, humans are the only species that consumes milk from another animal. Thousands of studies have been conducted on the harmful effects of dairy. But two big problems stand out: mucus and inflammation. Dairy causes the body to secrete too much mucus and in turn, the body then tries to get rid of the mucus through phlegm or acne. This over-abundance of mucus leads to inflammation within the body, which then leads to low energy, poor sleep, irregular digestion – and it can even cause diseases. If cutting back or eliminating dairy from your diet flags the question about getting enough calcium then consider eating more dark, leafy green vegetables. After all, this is where cows get their calcium. Statistically speaking, osteoporosis and hip fractures are actually lower and practically non-existent in countries with the lowest rate of dairy consumption.

On the plus side, there are some amazing plant-based milks out there finally. The variety, which ranges from almond to quinoa to oat to coconut, is amazing and they are far healthier than animal-based milk. When I first switched my entire family to plant-based alternatives, I bought every variety I could get my hands on and did a taste test to find out who preferred what. Try it, it works!

PROCESSED AND PACKAGED FOODS

Just like refined sugar, processed and packaged foods are dangerously addictive. And just like sugar and dairy, these 'junk' foods cause inflammation. But the really unfortunate fact is that these foods are pumped with nasty additives in order to boost taste and shelf-life. Remember, additives are chemicals and chemicals are free radicals. As we already know, free radicals damage cells. Processed foods have been stripped of their enzymes, vitamins and natural fibres in order for them to stay on the shelf longer, but in turn they wreak havoc in your body. Real, whole foods rot and decompose over time unlike processed 'junk' foods that remain unaltered while living on a shelf for months or even years!

What we want to do is be flexible. I totally get it that we will grab that jar of tomato or curry sauce when we're in a rush or exhausted and need something quick. We just need to balance it out with foods that are real and whole and make us feel great.

SUGAR

Refined sugar is in practically every processed and packaged food out there. It is addictive and creates cravings, low energy and bad moods. At first bite it spikes our blood sugar and we feel happy and alive. But just as quickly, it leaves us exhausted, ravenous and gloomy. So, what do we do? We end up eating more of it and the cycle continues.

Refined sugar also triggers the production of excess insulin, which drives our cells to store fat. If that's not enough to put you off sugar, then consider that it causes inflammation within the body. Inflammation has been shown to contribute to a number of diseases such as cancer, diabetes and digestion problems. We will be introducing a number of amazing sugar alternatives that are not only sweet to taste and help kick that addictive sugar craving, but are also filled with amazing nutrients to please your body and keep your mind balanced.

DON'T FRET!

Don't berate yourself if you do consume that steak, milkshake, meringue or bag of crisps occasionally. When you do, you know you can counteract that with foods that our bodies truly want and need. Vegetables and fruits contain thousands of nutrients with superhero health powers. These vegetables and fruits along with wholegrains, legumes and natural sweeteners are full of fibre, protein, iron and calcium, to name just a few. By decreasing our intake of meat, dairy, sugar and processed foods, we can reach a new level of health and well-being that we never expected we could enjoy.

REMEMBER THAT BY INTRODUCING MORE SUPERFOODS, YOU WILL NATURALLY CROWD OUT THE BAD STUFF.

THE GOLDEN RULES

There are 75 trillion cells within the body and they all work very hard to keep us going. The nutrients from the food we eat is absorbed by every single one of these cells. In order to maximise our health, we must maximise what nutrients get absorbed so that we can feel great every day. You do not need to go on some crazy diet to start feeling great. In fact, I'm not sure if there is a fad diet out there that actually makes you feel good – it seems to me that most of them make you feel pretty gloomy. I've come up with some Golden Rules to feeling great every day. Start following these and there's no reason why you can't keep having those chocolate biscuits every so often.

1 **Increase wholegrains**
From quinoa to bulghur wheat to brown rice to wholewheat pasta to soba noodles – get it in your everyday diet. Wholegrains are a wonderful source of nutrition. The body absorbs wholegrains slowly and therefore they deliver slow-releasing energy. And because wholegrains contain fibre, they help to control blood sugar and blood cholesterol, make you feel full so you eat less, and aid in the prevention of constipation.

2 **Increase sweet vegetables**
From corn to carrots to beetroot to squash to sweet potatoes – these guys really do help to crowd out the not-so-healthy foods in your diet. If you're somewhat dependent on refined sugar to sate your sugar cravings, not only are sweet vegetables packed with a superhighway of nutrients, but they appeal to that sweet tooth, too.

3 **Increase dark, leafy green vegetables**
From kale to spinach to romaine lettuce to pak choi, dark leafy green vegetables are crammed with goodness. Yet what's the food that's most missing in the modern day diet? Bingo! It's dark, leafy greens. From blood purification to improved circulation to a strengthened immune system to elevated moods, the benefits of these greens are too valuable to ignore. Whether you consume them through juicing to smoothies, or mains, side dishes or snacks, make a point to include them every single day.

4 **Increase good fats**
From avocados to coconuts to nuts and seeds – these fats are your friends. We need these particular friends for brain function, joint protection and energy. Even more so than carbohydrates or proteins, good fats are the greatest energy source and more energy helps to boost the metabolism.

5 **Increase legumes and beans**
From chickpeas to mung beans to lentils to black beans – this food group is a superior plant-based protein source. There are so many varieties out there and they are so versatile that you will never tire of them. I certainly haven't!

6 Decrease your refined sugar

From starving the brain to fuelling inflammation to ageing the skin to upsetting hormones, refined sugar has been chemically processed and literally stripped of all beneficial nutrients. Yuck. Check out dates, coconut palm sugar, honey and maple syrup instead to get a wholesome, nutrient-rich dose of the sweet stuff.

7 Decrease refined oil

The process of refining oil is equivalent to the refining of sugar and wholewheat into white foods. Think of it this way – it's taking a perfectly good food chock-full of its natural occurring vitamins, minerals and enzymes and stripping those goodies out. Banish the vegetable oil, safflower oil and sunflower oil once and for all.

8 Experiment with non-dairy alternatives

Plant-based milks are a great alternative to cows' milk. Free from all cholesterol and lactose (the sugar in animal milk), these non-dairy alternatives are plentiful in fatty acids and bursting with vitamins and minerals. Nowadays, there is a huge variety including almond, quinoa, coconut, rice, oat and hazelnut to name a few. Go on, take the plunge!

9 Experiment with the superfood superheroes

Certain superfood superheroes are the most impressive, almighty, super-condensed and nutrient-rich foods in the world. From improving overall well-being to reducing inflammation to boosting the immune system and alkalising the body, these superheroes nourish us deep within. Unleash your inner superhero by experimenting with cacao, goji berries, baobab, spirulina, bee pollen and yes, even sea vegetables.

10 Eat less meat, dairy, sugar and packaged or processed foods

These foods are cleverly designed to switch on the indulgent headquarters in our brain and brainwash us into making bad food choices. So, what's the simple solution? Eat more plants. I know that may sound daunting, but the tenth Golden Rule is not about taking it all away – it's about a willingness to come aboard a new adventure and experiment, dig in and bring back whole foods in their natural state. Amen.

RESTOCKING YOUR PANTRY

I want to make sure that you have healthy and nutritious foods on hand at all times so that you never come home and say, 'there's nothing to eat'. Which often means that you grab something incredibly unhealthy and usually don't feel so great afterwards. I don't want you to feel daunted by the amount of ingredients to have in your pantry, because in reality the list isn't exhaustive. In fact, I've made it manageable so that you can choose which of these items you want to get. If you need guidance, I've dropped them into three categories:

MUST translates as: 'Yes, you should definitely have this in your pantry, so go out and get it!'

SHOULD translates as: 'Well, I do advise it as it is a goodie!'

And **COULD** translates as: 'I'm not insisting – it's just another healthy option to have on hand.'

Having most of these items in stock will help support your new-found healthy eating habits and reduce the guilty temptations. Not only have I organised them into lists, but there is also a short explanation for each of them, explaining their healthy advantage.

MUST

WHOLEGRAINS

It's great to have a variety of wholegrains on hand because not only is their shelf life anywhere from six to nine months, but these guys make some super-filling, nutrient-rich and energy-boosting meals.

BROWN RICE (1)

Because it still has its bran layer unharmed (as opposed to stripped like white rice), brown rice retains all its naturally occurring nutrients, such as iron, manganese, selenium, magnesium and fibre. Out of all the grains, brown rice contains the highest amount of B vitamins. And as a bonus, brown rice is also gluten free.

QUINOA (2)

Out of all the wholegrains (in fact, it's a seed), quinoa has the greatest nutritional résumé. And it cooks the fastest out of all the grains, too. But what's so wonderful about quinoa is that it contains all eight amino acids, which makes it a complete protein.

ROLLED OATS (3)

These guys are so easy to ignore, but they boast a huge nutritional profile. Just 90g of these pale, small grains provide 6g protein and 4g fibre. And manganese – a mineral that helps to create enzymes for bone building – is found in abundance in this little grain. It's a totally affordable and nutrient-dense grain that can be used in so many different ways.

WHOLEGRAIN FLOURS

Here's my advice: go through your pantry right now and through away all white flour. I promise you, you don't need it ever again. White wheat flour is highly refined, therefore it has been stripped of its fibre, fatty acids, minerals and vitamins. You can still make amazing, delicious and more interesting treats by using wholegrain flours, which aren't devoid of their natural nutrients.

WHOLEMEAL/WHOLEGRAIN FLOUR (4)

This form of wheat flour contains the entire kernel of the grain, from the bran to the endosperm to the germ, which means we keep all the vitamins and fibre in our baking.

OAT FLOUR (5)

Here's your totally affordable grain in flour form. It is so versatile and packed with health, which makes it a winner for baking with.

BEANS

Beans are full of protein and very filling, making them a great substitute for meat in meals. They are low in fat and high in dietary fibre, and come in a massive variety of shapes, textures and flavours.

CHICKPEAS (6)

Chickpeas are great for digestive health. Consuming a small amount each day can also lower levels of bad cholesterol and improve heart health. The antioxidant composition of chickpeas is complex and valuable, providing a serious boost of goodness.

LENTILS (RED, BROWN AND PUY) (7)

There are several different varieties of lentils available, with the most common being red, brown and Puy. Lentils are an amazing source of protein and carbohydrates, and also contain impressive levels of calcium, iron, phosphorous and many B vitamins.

SEEDS AND NUTS

There's so much to write about nuts and seeds because they are high in everything! From protein to calcium to iron and folic acid, these little powerhouses pack a nutritional punch. However, you don't need a lot to reap the benefits – a small handful is ideal.

WALNUTS (8)

Possibly my favourite nut because they contain high amounts of omega 3 fatty acids. In fact, a 32g serving of walnuts contains over 90 percent of the recommended daily allowance of these fatty acids. In addition, walnuts are special because the fats in them are predominantly polyunsaturated, whereas most other nuts typically contain high amounts of monounsaturated fats.

ALMONDS (9)

Almonds are actually the seed of a stone fruit, related to apricots and peaches. Out of all the nuts, almonds are the highest in calcium and fibre. Countless studies have shown that eating these wonderful nuts regulates blood sugar, lowers cholesterol and can even assist with weight loss.

PUMPKIN SEEDS (10)

The seed of our friend the pumpkin, they are a fantastic source of the amino acid tryptophan, which is converted into serotonin – and remember, serotonin is nature's sleeping aid. So, perhaps it's a good idea to have a handful of these before you head off to bed at night.

CHIA SEEDS (11)

Hands down my favourite seed and here's why: simply consume 1 tablespoon of chia seeds a day and you've treated your body to more calcium than a cup of milk, more omega 3s than a piece of salmon, and more antioxidants than a handful of blueberries.

BUTTERS

Choosing dairy-free alternatives to butter is not only simple because of the range of options to choose from, but is also an incredible choice for optimum health. Plant-based butters are high in nutrients, whereas dairy-based alternatives are high in saturated fat and cholesterol.

ALMOND BUTTER (12)

Almond butter contains high levels of unsaturated fat, which is great for the heart health. The high omega-3 count also contributes to the optimum health of your heart, and will also help to protect you against strokes and certain diseases. When you eat almond butter, you are supplying your body with a wealth of potassium, magnesium, iron, calcium, phosphorous and also a generous helping of vitamin E!

SEA VEGETABLES

Considered the single most nutritious food on the planet, sea vegetables are packed with all the minerals we need for good health. Even though it is one of the world's most plentiful foods, it is one of the most wasted and underused. So let's get more sea vegetables into our diets by simply incorporating them in soups, salads and stir-fries.

NORI (13)

Out of all the seaweeds, not only is nori the easiest to digest, it also contains the highest amount of protein.

DULSE FLAKES (14)

Incredibly high in iron, dulse flakes are also a fantastic substitute for table salt for those looking to cut down or cut out, as dulse enhances the flavour and saltiness of your meals. This flake is your friend.

DRIED FRUIT AND NATURAL SWEETENERS

Why restock your pantry with natural sweeteners? Well, if you haven't heard, white sugar (and even brown sugar) has pretty much all its built-in vitamins and minerals stripped away. When these vitamins and minerals are removed, it wreaks havoc on your blood sugar levels and causes 'sugar blues' because your body needs these very nutrients to help metabolise the sugar you eat.

RAISINS (15)

These little gems are a great boost of energy when you're feeling sluggish because of their natural sugars, and are also a high source of dietary fibre to keep things moving in the digestive tract. Plus, they are super-high in a trace mineral called boron, which is important for healthy bones as it converts vitamin D to its active form, and without vitamin D, we can't absorb calcium effectively.

DATES (16)

Dates contain too many vitamins, minerals and phytonutrients to list, so let's just say that even though they aren't the prettiest foods to look at, they are definitely worth eating for overall well-being.

COCONUT PALM SUGAR (17)

Offering more vitamins, minerals and phytonutrients than refined sugar, coconut palm sugar is also very low on the glycemic index – ranking at 35 compared to sugar, which ranks between 60 and 75. It is easy to replace sugar in your cooking, as coconut palm sugar can be substituted, gram for gram, for refined sugar.

CONDIMENTS

The things we add to our meals have the potential to either add extra nutrition or to compromise the healthy status of a dish. By choosing condiments that are beneficial to optimum health, we are able to add flavour to mealtimes whilst also doing the best for our bodies.

APPLE CIDER VINEGAR (18)

The potential long-term benefits of including apple cider vinegar in your diet range from weight loss to preventing heart disease. It is also great for controlling blood sugar levels.

MUSTARD (19)

This popular condiment is the combination of mustard seeds, water, vinegar and a selection of spices and flavourings. It is low in calories and high in selenium, which has antioxidant properties that protect the cells from damage. Mustard is also a good source of omega-3 fatty acids, which are essential for the health of your brain tissue.

FRESH GINGER (20)

This immune-boosting food is most commonly known for its ability to fight colds and flu. Ginger also has effective anti-inflammatory properties and will add an aromatic flavour when used in cooking. Vitamins B6, E and C are the most prominent vitamins found in ginger, alongside a long list of minerals. Due to its strong medicinal qualities, it has been used in China for over 2,000 years to treat various ailments.

FRESH GARLIC (21)

In large doses, garlic can provide some serious health benefits to the circulatory system, as well as protecting against certain cancers. However, when consumed in small, regular doses, garlic will still contribute to all-round good health. It is low in fat, completely free of cholesterol and will help your body to absorb calcium from other sources.

VANILLA EXTRACT (22)

Vanilla extract is the liquid form of the vanilla bean and is used both in cooking and for medicinal purposes. It is rumoured to have aphrodisiac properties and is most popularly used to flavour a variety of drinks and baked goods. It contains trace amounts of essential minerals and is especially high in potassium, which helps to control blood pressure and heart rate.

OILS

I'm afraid that not all oils are created equal. So it's essential to get rid of any unrefined oils and replace them with a few healthy, refined oils. I've only listed a few, as frankly only a few oils are needed for all your cooking needs. The oils I've listed help our metabolism to function effectively and feed our skin, hair and nails.

COCONUT OIL (23)

From maintaining a healthy heart and fighting infection, to improving digestion and metabolism and even promoting healthy skin and hair, coconut oil is the mother of all oils in my book. Because it doesn't breakdown at high temperatures, it's fantastic for most of your cooking needs.

OLIVE OIL (24)

Make sure you buy unfiltered, first cold-pressed olive oil (extra-virgin), as it retains more nutrients than the filtered variety. Olive oil contains heart-healthy antioxidants, but if it gets heated too high, these beneficial compounds start to deteriorate. So, it's best to use olive oil in a salad dressing, or only cook with it over a low to medium heat.

SPICES AND HERBS

Incorporating spices into cooking is the best way to add flavour and nutrition to a meal at the same time. Just a dash of spice can make a dull dish more exciting for the taste buds and more beneficial for the body.

TURMERIC (25)

This spice has a bitter but warm flavour and is most commonly used to make curry. It has long been used medicinally for its anti-inflammatory properties, and in Chinese medicine to treat depression. Recent research has also shown it to be a strong antioxidant that can help to control cholesterol levels.

CINNAMON (26)

This sweet spice boasts one of the highest known antioxidant strengths and is an excellent source of vitamins and minerals. One teaspoon of ground cinnamon has as much antioxidant strength as a cup of pomegranate juice or half a cup of blueberries. It has strong anti-inflammatory and antiseptic properties and can help with digestive health.

CAYENNE PEPPER (27)

Cayenne pepper has been used throughout history for detoxing regimes, as it stimulates the circulatory and digestive systems and neutralizes acidity in the body.

CUMIN (28)
Cooking with ground cumin is a fantastic way to get magnesium into your body. Magnesium is essential for optimum heart health as well as helpful for controlling blood pressure. Cumin is also a rich source of iron, which your body needs to carry oxygen to the cells.

PAPRIKA (29)
Paprika will add a vibrant red tint to a dish. It is loaded with carotenoids, which are fantastic for eye health. It is also extremely high in vitamin A, which is essential for a healthy immune system and cell growth.

SUPERFOOD SUPERHEROES

These are possibly my favourite foods to write and talk about. Granted, I could list a whole bunch more, but for the recipes included in this book, the superheroes listed below have the winning combination of being easier to find, easier to incorporate into recipes and yet still are super nutrient-dense. At first glance, superfoods might seem quite pricey, but bear in mind that you only need a pinch to get a huge shot of nutrients.

GOJI BERRIES (30)
Known as the secret to longevity and strengthening the immune system in Chinese medicine, goji berries contain 18 amino acids, including the eight essential ones, and an incredible amount of antioxidants.

CACAO POWDER (31)
Chocolate – we all love it. But cacao is KING as it has not been toasted, roasted or cooked, like cocoa, therefore retaining all the original health benefits. Cacao is one of the most antioxidant-rich foods on the planet, as well as being one of the best plant-based sources of magnesium, which helps to keep us relaxed.

BAOBAB POWDER (32)
The newest superfood from Africa to hit the market is baobab. It is denser in iron than red meat, denser in vitamin C than oranges, and is a great source of calcium, potassium and magnesium.

SPIRULINA (33)
Touted as the original 'superfood', this blue-green algae is so nutrient dense you could survive on just spirulina and water alone. Tons of studies have been carried out to prove spirulina's status as THE nutrient powerhouse. It contains about 60 percent protein and all the eight essential amino acids, plus a high chlorophyll content, making it a great detoxifier. Simply put, spirulina is one of the most nutritious food sources in the world.

BEE POLLEN (34)
Bee pollen is now being recognised as one of the world's most complete foods as it contains nearly all the nutrients you need. It is more abundant in proteins than any other animal source and, gram for gram, it contains more amino acids than beef, eggs or cheese.

AÇAÍ BERRY (35)
The red grapes used to make wine consist of a compound called anthocyanin, which is high in antioxidants. The açaí berry includes these particular antioxidants but has up to 30 times that amount.

SHOULD

WHOLEGRAINS

PEARL BARLEY (1)
This is packed with fibre, so it's wonderful to use in place of arborio rice when making risotto, as it absorbs flavours just as readily as rice. It's also cholesterol free and has less than 1g fat per serving.

BUCKWHEAT AND SOBA NOODLES (2)
Buckwheat stays in the digestive tract the longest out of all wholegrains (in fact, it's a seed), making it the most filling. This grain is actually a relative of rhubarb and is famously known for stabilising blood sugar – it is therefore a very good grain for diabetics. Soba noodles are made from buckwheat flour, which makes both the grain and the noodle gluten free.

WHOLEGRAIN FLOURS

COCONUT FLOUR (3)
Made from dried coconut meat, this flour is a great source of lauric acid, which supports the immune system and thyroid, as well as promoting healthy skin.

BEANS

BLACK BEANS (4)
Research has shown that the colon benefits from a diet rich in black beans because of their effect on good bacteria growth. They are also incredibly low calorie, whilst also being high in fibre and carbohydrates, making them the perfect energising food.

EDAMAME (5)
Edamame are made from soya beans that haven't reached full maturity yet. They are a fantastic source of dietary fibre, protein, omega fatty acids and carbohydrates, as well as containing many other vitamins and minerals. They are one of the few plant-based foods that contain all nine essential amino acids and make a great snack between meals.

SEEDS AND NUTS

PINE NUTS (6)
Yet another seed that's called a nut, pine nuts are actually the seed of the pine cone. They are rich in magnesium and in a fatty acid called pinoelic acid, which has been proven to aid in weight loss. Again, there is no need to overindulge as a small handful is enough to get a big nutritional boost.

SESAME SEEDS (7)
An excellent source of copper, which is essential to the functioning of our organs and efficient metabolism, sesame seeds also contain two distinctive substances: sesamin and sesamolin, both of which help to lower cholesterol.

FLAXSEEDS (8)
A truly extraordinary source of omega-3 fatty acids, which, amongst a host of other benefits, help to calm any inflammation in the body. However, the body can only take advantage of these fats when the seeds are ground. So my advice is to buy ground flaxseeds to save the hassle of grinding them yourself. As they are so high in these fats, flaxseeds need to be stored in the fridge or freezer, or they will spoil very quickly.

HEMP SEEDS (9)
Just like flaxseeds, hemp seeds contain a high amount of omega-3 fatty acids, but for those who avoid animal products, hemp seeds are a great alternative, as they contain a very high amount of quality protein, too.

BUTTERS

TAHINI (10)

Tahini is made from ground sesame seeds and comes in two forms, either hulled (light) or unhulled (dark). Hulled tahini loses many of its nutrients during the production process whereas the seeds in unhulled tahini are mostly left intact. Unhulled tahini is rich in minerals, such as phosphorous, lecithin and magnesium, as well as being a great source of methionine, which helps to detoxify the liver.

NON-DAIRY MILKS

There are several reasons people opt for non-dairy alternatives to regular milk. These days, there is such an incredible range available and most are packed with essential nutrients, vitamins and minerals. As well as being much better for health than dairy milk, these alternatives also have a much longer shelf life and come in a variety of flavours.

OAT MILK (11)

Oat milk is a high folic-acid, high-fibre alternative to dairy milk that will reduce bad cholesterol levels. Oats are known to enhance the immune system, whilst also protecting against cardiovascular diseases. They make for a tasty drink in this form, too.

COCONUT MILK (12)

This amazingly nutritious dairy alternative is made from the flesh of the coconut. It contains an abundance of vitamins B, C and E, as well as being rich in iron, phosphorous, potassium and magnesium.

ALMOND MILK (13)

This is a fantastic dairy-free option for those who are allergic to soy. It has a nutty, creamy flavour and is quite simple to make at home. Almond milk is the perfect choice for those who are looking after their heart, as it contains absolutely no cholesterol or saturated fat.

DRIED FRUIT AND NATURAL SWEETENERS

APRICOTS (14)

Often overlooked, apricots are one of my favourite dried fruits as they are low in calories, and high in fibre, vitamin C and vitamin A, which, amongst other benefits, is good for your eyesight.

MAPLE SYRUP (15)

Lower on the glycemic index than refined sugar, maple syrup boasts up to 54 different antioxidants – double the amount previously thought. Replace 200g sugar with about 120ml maple syrup.

RAW HONEY (16)

Most honey is heated thus destroying some of its enzymes, antioxidants and antibacterial properties. Raw honey has an impressive and exceptional nutritional value. Replace 200g sugar with about 120ml or 160g honey.

CONDIMENTS

SAUERKRAUT (17)

This traditional German dish, made from cabbage, boasts some serious health benefits due to the good bacteria that are produced as it is made. As cabbage ferments, live, friendly bacteria grow and combat any bad bacteria as it enters your digestive system. It is also full of fibre and a wealth of vitamins K and C. However, it is fairly high in sodium, so enjoy in moderation.

OLIVES (18)

Olives are naturally delicious and have such a variety of health benefits that eating them everyday is a great idea. They can stimulate the digestive system, reduce bad cholesterol in the body and help to control blood sugar. Added to this, they are a good source of dietary fibre and antioxidants, plus a range of essential minerals. They are incredibly affordable, especially when bought in bulk.

OILS

FLAXSEED OIL (19)
The '3' in omega-3 fatty acids refers to the 3 big hitters that are absorbed from foods. Flaxseed oil, in particular, contains a high amount of one of these: alpha-linoleic acid (ALA). For years, ALA was overlooked, but the health benefits associated with ALA are finally bringing it, and flaxseed, into the spotlight.

SPICES AND HERBS

BASIL (20)
Basil is bursting with phytonutrients, which nourish the body and help to combat disease. It contains exceptionally high amounts of vitamin A and beta-carotene, which are both effective at fighting free radicals in the body.

MUSTARD SEEDS (21)
Mustard seeds are a great source of both selenium and magnesium, making them useful in reducing the symptoms of conditions like asthma and arthritis. They are perfect for use as a condiment and a cooking ingredient.

BAY LEAF (22)
This herb is a tasty way to season curry and soup dishes, but also has powerful medicinal properties that combat infection and heal wounds. Bay leaves can be used in fresh, dried or powdered form, but are most commonly used as dried whole leaves.

TAMARI (23)
Made from fermented soya beans, tamari is similar in flavour and texture to soy sauce. However, it is generally richer and thicker, and contains less salt than soy sauce does. Furthermore, it is usually gluten free, unlike soy sauce. Tamari is a delicious source of niacin, protein, manganese and also tryptophan, making it a healthy addition to the dining table.

COULD

WHOLEGRAINS

MILLET (1)
Super-high in magnesium, potassium, iron, fibre and protein, this ancient grain has been around for thousands of years. Personally, I like it because it contains silica – which helps to strengthen skin, hair and nails. And it's gluten free, too.

BULGHUR WHEAT (2)
Bulghur wheat is made by par-cooking and coarsely grinding wheat berries. It is rich in protein and minerals and serves as a great alternative to rice or pasta.

WHOLEGRAIN FLOURS

BUCKWHEAT FLOUR (3)
You already know that buckwheat is good for you as a grain. But as flour, I love it even more as it can be used to make amazing pancakes, cupcakes and breads.

SPELT FLOUR (4)
Spelt is an ancient grain and a distant cousin of wheat that is easier to digest that wheat itself. It boasts an exceptional mineral content, including iron and magnesium, and spelt flour can be easily substituted for wheat in many recipes.

QUINOA FLOUR (5)
Just like the quinoa grain, this flour contains more protein than any of the other flours. It is a gluten-free flour that has a slightly nutty flavour and is great for biscuits, cakes, pasta and bread.

BEANS

ADZUKI (6)
These beans are a reddish brown colour and have a sweet, nut-like flavour. They are most commonly used in Asian cuisine and are especially popular in Japan for their health-boosting properties. They are high in soluble fibre as well as a range of nutrients, such as riboflavin, niacin, thiamine and potassium.

CANNELLINI (7)
Cannellini beans are an excellent high-fibre, low-calorie source of protein, and they supply the body with beneficial complex carbohydrates. These beans are also packed with potassium, zinc, iron and many other essential vitamins and minerals.

TOFU (8)
Tofu is a great way for vegetarians and vegans to get their fill of protein and it's the perfect accompaniment to a low-fat, low-calorie diet. Tofu itself doesn't have much flavour, but it will easily absorb the flavours of the foods, spices or herbs that you cook it with.

SEEDS AND NUTS

CASHEWS (9)
These nuts are bursting with vitamins, minerals and fibre, but are especially high in the heart-healthy monounsaturated fat, oleic acid. This essential fatty acid helps to lower bad LDL cholesterol and increase the good HDL cholesterol. Beware not to overindulge though, as 100g cashews equals 550 calories.

BRAZIL NUTS (10)
What makes Brazil nuts stand out, is the incredibly high amount of selenium they contain. Selenium increases your body's ability to fight off free radicals, as well as maintaining a healthy thyroid. Just one to two Brazil nuts a day supplies your body with enough of this trace element.

SUNFLOWER SEEDS (11)
The superstar in these small seeds is no doubt vitamin E with its antioxidant properties. Not only does vitamin E help with arthritic pain but it also keeps your skin youthful as vitamin E protects against UV rays.

BUTTERS

HAZELNUT BUTTER (12)
Made from crushed and blended hazelnuts, this butter is high in natural fats as well as essential vitamins and minerals. It also contains high levels of phytosterols, which are one of the most powerful antioxidant types. Although it is high in calories, a small amount of hazelnut butter will soon have you feeling full.

CACAO BUTTER (13)
This butter comes directly from chocolate! It's the pure, cold-pressed oil that comes from the cacao bean, which is the source of all cocoa products. A wonderful ingredient to use for a healthy chocolate sauce.

SEA VEGETABLES

WAKAME (14)
This is the seaweed most commonly used in miso soup. Not only is wakame high on the nutrition charts, but it's also incredibly low calorie and is said to actually help burn fat.

KOMBU (15)
If you cook your beans, rather than buy them in a tin, then kombu is the perfect seaweed to aid in the digestion of beans. Kombu contains glutamic acid, which helps to break down the hard-to-digest sugars in beans.

NON-DAIRY MILKS

SOY MILK (16)
This is definitely the most popular alternative to dairy milk, as it's very high in protein. Soy milk is often fortified with B12, which is a vitamin that only occurs naturally in animal products. Drinking this kind of milk will provide the body with a variety of essential nutrients and antioxidants.

RICE MILK (17)
This is the most hypoallergenic of the milks mentioned and is the best alternative for those who have to avoid dairy, soy and nuts. Similarly to almond milk, it also contains no saturated fat or cholesterol, and it is also a great source of essential B vitamins. Rice milk also boasts a great antioxidant count and can do wonders for the immune system.

DRIED FRUIT AND NATURAL SWEETENERS

CURRANTS (18)
A relative of the raisin, currants have a very similar antioxidant and nutrient profile. Remember, antioxidants help fight off and prevent free-radical damage in the body.

CRANBERRIES (19)
Aside from blueberries, cranberries trump nearly every fruit and vegetable in the antioxidant department – that includes strawberries, raspberries, cherries and even spinach and broccoli! They are very high in vitamin C, too.

BROWN RICE SYRUP (20)
Yes, it is actually made from brown rice that has been soaked, then sprouted and cooked with an enzyme to help break it down. I like it because its fructose free and low on the glycemic index, and therefore won't spike your blood sugar like refined white and brown sugar does. Replace 200g sugar with 240–315ml brown rice syrup.

CONDIMENTS

UMEBOSHI PLUMS (21)
These pickled Japanese plums have a host of medicinal qualities. Consuming them will stimulate digestion, combat fatigue and also help to eliminate toxins. They are also said to be an effective hangover cure and one of the best preventative medicine foods available.

CAPERS (22)
Capers are the pickled flower buds from the Mediterranean caper bush. They are picked fresh, then preserved in either brine, salt or wine vinegar. Even though they are small, they are hugely flavourful and nutritious. They are especially good for red blood cell health due to their high iron count.

SUN-DRIED TOMATOES (23)
Low in calories and fat but high in nutrients, these are a tasty addition to meals. In this form, tomatoes are especially high in dietary fibre, potassium, copper and vitamin C.

NUTRITIONAL YEAST (24)
If you don't eat any animal products, then one crucial nutrient you need to get elsewhere is vitamin B12 and luckily nutritional yeast contains a lot of it. In fact, 1 tablespoon a day provides you with the RDA of B12.

MATCHA GREEN TEA (25)
A powdered version of green tea, but much more potent; 1 cup of matcha tea has ten times the amount of antioxidants in green or black tea and, gram for gram, has ten to 20 times the amount of antioxidants in blueberries, açaí berries or pomegranates.

HIMALAYAN SEA SALT (26)
This is a healthy pink salt from the Himalayan mountain range and thought to be the purest salt on earth. Its colour is indicative of its high count of at least 80 minerals. Amazingly, it is known to increase hydration, lower blood pressure and improve circulation.

GARLIC POWDER (27)

This is made by dehydrating and grinding up garlic cloves. It has a comparable nutritional composition to raw garlic and has been used throughout history both medicinally and in cooking.

SPICES AND HERBS

MARJORAM (28)

This is one of the most popular of the Mediterranean herbs and has been utilised in cooking and medicine for thousands of years. It has a mildly spicy but sweet flavour and contains high levels of vitamin C.

CARAWAY SEEDS (29)

These aromatic seeds contain a huge range of health benefiting minerals, nutrients, antioxidants and minerals. They are great for digestive health due, to their high dietary fibre count, and also have anti-flatulent properties.

FENNEL SEEDS (30)

Fennel seeds can be purchased whole or ground to a powder and have been used medicinally to aid digestion. It's always best to store fennel seeds in an airtight container in the fridge as they can quickly lose their flavour otherwise. They contain an abundance of vital B vitamins, as well as vitamins A, E and C.

ROSEMARY (31)

Rosemary is a herb that is particularly rich in B vitamins, such as riboflavin and folic acid. It also has high levels of folates, which are great for pregnant women as they help to prevent neural tube defects forming. Vitamins A and C are also prevalent in rosemary, alongside a selection of minerals and iron.

SAGE (32)

This herb is widely acknowledged as a natural remedy. It is used medicinally to treat a range of ailments, and is especially useful for those suffering from fevers or irregular sleeping patterns. Sage can be used in cooking, in teas and also in capsule form as a supplement.

THYME (33)

Thyme is one of the most popular herbs for cooking with and has numerous health boosting properties. Selenium, manganese, magnesium, calcium, iron and potassium can all be found in thyme leaves. As with most herbs, it's best to cook with fresh thyme and you can easily grow it at home.

OREGANO (34)

Oregano is a herb that features prominently in the heart-healthy Mediterranean diet. The leaves have an aromatic but slightly bitter taste, which adds a complex flavour when used in cooking. Oregano is an excellent source of vitamin C, potassium, magnesium and calcium.

CUMIN SEEDS (35)

This spice has a slightly nutty flavour and is particularly fragrant in whole seed form, rather than ready ground. It features in Indian and Middle Eastern cooking for its taste as well as its nutritional perks. It contains an abundance of iron and is known to support the digestive system. Studies also suggest that it has anti-carcinogenic properties.

SUPERFOOD SUPERHEROES

LUCUMA (36)

A great alternative sweetener, lucuma powder is made from the fruit of the lucuma tree in South America. Unlike most artificial sweeteners that offer no nutritional value, lucuma is a wonderful natural sweetener rich in fibre, and crucially, it does not spike your blood sugar levels.

BREAKFAST

The word 'breakfast' literally means to take a break from your fast, as it's the first meal taken after a night's sleep. It is incredibly important to nourish yourself in the morning after a night of fasting – you will have much more energy and perform much better throughout the day. If you want to boost your metabolism, then eating breakfast is one of the best and fastest ways to do so. And remember, skipping meals, especially breakfast, often leads to over-eating later in the day. A great way to get into the habit of eating a healthy, nutritious and energy-boosting breakfast is to plan your meal before you go to bed at night. For example, when I know I want a green smoothie in the morning, I put all the ingredients in my blender the night before. The following day, I'm usually woken by the sound of the blender as my 16-year-old daughter, Emma, has already turned it on and is drinking it herself. She loves green smoothies, too!

SIMPLE GRANOLA WITH PUMPKIN SEEDS AND GOJI BERRIES

GREEN AÇAÍ BERRY BOWL

Sadly, most shop-bought granola is packed with sugar. In fact, if you look on the pack, you will usually see that sugar is either the second or third ingredient listed on the back. When you make your own granola at home, you're in control of the amount of goodness that goes in and you can experiment with different nuts, seeds and flavours. **(See photograph on page 34.)**

90g rolled oats
170g buckwheat groats
60g walnuts, chopped
35g pumpkin seeds
55g goji berries
2 tablespoons raw honey
2 tablespoons coconut palm sugar
2 tablespoons coconut oil

Serves 4–6

Preheat the oven to 180°C/Gas 4. Melt the coconut oil in a saucepan over a low heat and let it cool. Once cooled, mix all the ingredients in a bowl using your hands. Spread the mixture thinly on a baking tray and bake in the preheated oven for 10 minutes, or until lightly toasted. Cool before serving or storing in a container in a cool, dry place.

In the last few years, green smoothies have been all the rage and I do still love them, but there's a new gang in town called the BOWL. It's much prettier and it's easy to add some delicious toppings.

1 banana (frozen if you
  want a cold bowl)
120ml coconut water
3 dates, pitted
Large handful of spinach
1 kiwi, peeled
1 teaspoon açaí powder
  (or more if you fancy!)

For the toppings
Raspberries
Coconut flakes
Bee pollen

Serves 1

Put all the ingredients in a blender or food processor and whizz away.

Top with raspberries, coconut flakes and bee pollen.

JUST 35G PUMPKIN SEEDS CONTAINS NEARLY HALF OF THE DAILY RECOMMENDED DOSE OF MAGNESIUM, WHICH HELPS OUR BODY TO RELAX.

NOT ONLY IS THE AÇAÍ BERRY HIGH IN ANTIOXIDANTS THAT HELP TO FIGHT FREE RADICALS, BUT IT'S FANTASTIC FOR YOUR DIGESTION, TOO.

Kids love sprinkles and decorations,
so they'll love this pretty but
wholesome breakfast bowl.

BUCKWHEAT PORRIDGE
WITH PAPAYA TOPPING

170g buckwheat groats
480ml water
120ml almond milk (or any
  plant-based milk)
1 teaspoon vanilla extract
1 tablespoon lime juice

For the papaya topping
1 large papaya
Zest of 1 lime
½ teaspoon ground cinnamon
¼ teaspoon ground ginger
¼ teaspoon ground nutmeg
2 tablespoons raw honey
2 tablespoons pumpkin seeds

Serves 2

At first glance, you might think this is going to
be a tricky recipe, but in reality it's quite easy –
especially when it comes to making the buckwheat
porridge. You can get most of this ready the night
before, which is a bonus, particularly if you're
rushing to work or doing the school run.

Soak the buckwheat groats in the 480ml water for
at least 1 hour or overnight. After soaking, strain
and rinse well. Put the soaked groats, almond milk,
vanilla extract and lime juice in a blender or food
processor and blitz well.

To make the topping, peel the papaya, then cut it
into chunks and place in a large jar or container.
Add the remaining ingredients and mash together
with a large spoon – this will release the juices from
the papaya, but be sure to leave a few good chunks.
Cover your jar or container with an airtight lid and
place in the fridge to marinate if you have time.
(Again, a great one to get ready the night before.)

Once marinated and ready to go, put your porridge
in a bowl and spoon the papaya topping all over.

IN ADDITION TO BEING HIGH IN VITAMINS
A AND C, PAPAYA CONTAINS PAPAIN,
A DIGESTIVE ENZYME THAT IS USED
TO TREAT DIGESTIVE DISORDERS. IT IS
ALSO EXCELLENT FOR SKIN CONDITIONS,
SUCH AS ACNE.

Try these moreish, health-giving pancakes and you'll never want to skip breakfast again.

CHIA AND COCONUT FLOUR PANCAKES WITH BLUEBERRY BAOBAB SAUCE

6 tablespoons chia seeds
270ml water
60g coconut oil, melted,
  plus extra for greasing
300ml almond milk
1 teaspoon vanilla extract
50g coconut palm sugar
100g coconut flour
100g buckwheat flour
1½ teaspoons baking powder
Maple syrup, for drizzling
  (optional)

For the blueberry baobab sauce
150g blueberries
100g coconut palm sugar
120ml water
2 tablespoons lemon juice
1 tablespoon xanthan gum
1 tablespoon baobab powder

Makes about 12 small pancakes

I wanted a new twist on the same old wholewheat pancakes that I had been making for years, so I decided to experiment. This recipe is a mixture of two nutritious flours: coconut flour and buckwheat flour. That means you are looking at some gluten-free pancakes that are bursting with health.

To make the blueberry baobab sauce, heat the blueberries, coconut palm sugar, 120ml water and lemon juice in a small saucepan. Stir frequently, then bring to a low boil. Use a fork to mash the blueberries to help release some of the juices. Slowly stir in the xanthun gum – this helps to thicken the sauce – and the baobab powder, then simmer until the blueberry sauce is thick enough. Leave to cool.

Combine the chia seeds with the 270ml water in a bowl and leave to soak for 20 minutes. Put the coconut oil, almond milk, vanilla and coconut palm sugar in a large bowl and add the chia seed mixture. Stir in the coconut flour, buckwheat flour and baking powder.

Grease a non-stick frying pan with coconut oil and heat over a medium heat. Pour one-quarter of a cup of batter into the pan for each pancake and cook for 2 minutes on the first side and 1 minute on the other, until they are golden brown. Don't be alarmed by how thick the batter is – this is due to the coconut flour.

To serve, stack the pancakes and smother with the blueberry sauce. Drizzle with maple syrup, if using.

CHIA SEEDS ARE GREAT AS AN EGG REPLACEMENT, AND, BECAUSE THEY SWELL TO UP TO 10 TIMES THEIR SIZE WHEN MIXED WITH LIQUID, YOU FEEL FULLER FOR LONGER.

CREAMY BREAKFAST BOWL WITH BASIL AND BLUEBERRIES

Handful of chopped, fresh coconut
½ banana
½ avocado, peeled, pitted and chopped
¼ cucumber
Handful of blueberries, plus extra to serve, if liked
2 dates, pitted
8 fresh basil leaves
Juice of 1 lime
2.5cm piece of fresh ginger
240ml coconut water
Desiccated coconut, to serve

Optional toppings
Bee pollen
Chia seeds
Goji berries

Serves 1

Don't worry; this one does not taste like a salad! It has some super greens hidden in it, along with avocado to give it that creamy texture. The blueberries create a lovely colour and help to mask the 'green', which is especially clever if you want to get your kids to eat this. And trust me, they will dive right in just like all my kids do as they simply love it.

Toss all the ingredients in a blender or food processor and whizz away.

Serve in a bowl, top with more blueberries and a sprinkle of desiccated coconut. For a real superfood boost, add the other optional toppings.

If you put all the ingredients in the blender or food processor the night before, when you wake up, you just have to switch it on and voilà... breakfast is served!

BASIL COMES FROM THE SAME FAMILY AS MINT AND IS TOUTED AS ONE OF THE HEALTHIEST HERBS DUE TO ITS IMPRESSIVE VITAMIN K COUNT, WHICH IS ESSENTIAL FOR BLOOD CLOTTING.

COCONUT AND ALMOND QUINOA WITH STEWED PLUMS

170g quinoa
600ml coconut milk (or any
  plant-based milk)
2 teaspoons ground cinnamon
1 teaspoon vanilla extract

For the stewed plums
4 tablespoons almond butter
  (or any other nut butter you
  have to hand)
6 medium plums
100g coconut palm sugar
240ml water
1 cinnamon stick

To serve
Raw honey, for drizzling
Desiccated coconut,
  for sprinkling

Serves 4

I get the same question all the time… quinoa for breakfast? And the answer is YES! It's so delicious and, just like porridge, it keeps you full for hours and energised throughout your morning. This combination of ingredients packs in the protein as well, due to the combination of quinoa and almond butter. I've made it nice and sweet, the healthy way, to get that sweet-tooth fix.

Combine the quinoa and coconut milk together in a medium saucepan and bring to the boil. Add the cinnamon and vanilla extract, cover and simmer on a low heat for 15–20 minutes.

Meanwhile, make the stewed plums. Cut the plums in half, remove the pits, then cut the plum halves into chunks. Combine the coconut palm sugar, 240ml water and cinnamon stick in saucepan over a medium to high heat and bring to the boil. Add the plums and continue to cook until the plums are tender. Once tender, use a fork to slightly mash.

Once the quinoa is cooked but still a bit runny, put it in 4 bowls and stir in 1 tablespoon of almond butter per bowl. Top with the stewed plums, a drizzle of honey and a sprinkle of desiccated coconut.

PLUMS ARE JUST AS HIGH IN ANTIOXIDANTS AND PHYTONUTRIENTS AS BLUEBERRIES. THE IMPORTANT THING IS TO NEVER PEEL YOUR PLUMS AS THE SKIN IS WHERE MANY OF THE ANTIOXIDANTS AND PHYTONUTRIENTS ARE HIDING.

BANANA FRENCH TOAST WITH COCONUT CREAM

300ml coconut milk (or any
  plant-based milk)
2 very ripe bananas, plus extra,
  sliced, to serve
1 tablespoon chia seeds
1 tablespoon ground flaxseed
½ teaspoon ground cinnamon
½ teaspoon ground nutmeg
½ teaspoon vanilla extract
Coconut oil, for greasing
8–10 slices of spelt bread

For the coconut cream
1 x 400ml tin of coconut milk
1 tablespoon maple syrup,
  plus extra to serve
½ vanilla pod

Serves 4–6

I remember many Saturdays waking up to my mum's perfect French toast in the States. I even preferred it to her perfect pancakes! It was such a winner that we'd sometimes be allowed to have it for supper, too. Here's a healthy twist on this yummy treat – perfect as a breakfast in bed for someone special.

Place the tin of coconut milk in the fridge the night before you make this recipe.

To make the coconut cream, scoop the cream out of the chilled tin of coconut milk and use the leftover water in a smoothie or soup. Place the coconut cream into a mixing bowl and add the maple syrup. Scrape the seeds from the vanilla pod into the mixture. Using a hand-held whisk, whip the cream until super fluffy.

To make the French toast, put the bananas in a food processor with the coconut milk, chia seeds, ground flaxseed, cinnamon, nutmeg and vanilla extract and blitz to a batter.

Coat a frying pan with coconut oil and set over a medium heat. Working in batches, dip the slices of spelt bread into the batter and let them soak for 5–10 seconds on either side. Using a fork, transfer the battered bread to your heated pan and cook for 3–4 minutes on each side, or until golden brown.

Serve immediately with the coconut cream topping, maple syrup and some more sliced banana.

WE ALL KNOW BANANAS ARE HIGH IN POTASSIUM, BUT ADDITIONALLY, THEY CONTAIN HIGH LEVELS OF TRYPTOPHAN, WHICH IS CONVERTED INTO SEROTONIN AND MAKES US HAPPY!

WILD MUSHROOMS ON SPELT TOAST

250g mixed fresh mushrooms
  (try oyster, shiitake or reishi)
2 tablespoons coconut oil
1 small onion, chopped
35g almonds, roughly chopped
2 garlic cloves, chopped
Handful of spinach
½ teaspoon cayenne pepper
½ teaspoon ground turmeric
2 slices of spelt bread, toasted
1 lemon, halved
Balsamic vinegar, for drizzling

Serves 4–6

This recipe is incredibly flexible because the mushrooms I've listed are just examples of the many different mushrooms you could use. So be adventurous and maybe try some other interesting varieties, as there are so many to choose from. (See photograph on page 49.)

Make sure you give your mushrooms a good clean first. Slice any large mushrooms but keep the small ones whole.

Heat the coconut oil in a frying pan until it melts, then add the chopped onion. Cook over a medium heat until the onion becomes translucent.

Add the mushrooms, coat them in the coconut oil and cook for 3 minutes, or until they begin to soften.

Add the almonds, garlic, spinach, cayenne pepper and turmeric and fry for several minutes. Remove from the heat and pile the mushroom mixture on top of toasted spelt bread.

Squeeze your lemon over the mushrooms and drizzle some balsamic vinegar over the top before serving.

MUSHROOMS ARE THE ONLY VEGETARIAN FOOD TO CONTAIN VITAMIN D. VITAMIN D DEFICIENCY IS ON THE RISE IN BRITAIN. AMONGST A HOST OF OTHER BENEFITS, WE NEED IT TO EFFECTIVELY ABSORB CALCIUM.

CHILLI AVOCADO MASH AND COCONUT OIL ON RYE

2 ripe avocados, peeled,
  pitted and chopped
2 spring onions, chopped
1 garlic clove, crushed
½ teaspoon sea salt
1 teaspoon dried chilli flakes
Juice of 1 lime
4 slices of rye bread
4 tablespoons coconut oil
Freshly ground black pepper

Serves 4

This is possibly my favourite breakfast of all time. But the great thing about this recipe is that it's perfect as a snack too. I love to slather coconut oil and avocado on pretty much everything. This recipe combines them both and adds some bonus ingredients to make it super healthy, super filling and super-energising.

Combine the ripe avocados, spring onions, garlic, sea salt, chilli flakes and lime juice in a small bowl and mash well using a fork.

Toast the rye bread and, while it is still warm, spread each piece with 1 tablespoon coconut oil.

Spoon the avocado mash evenly on each piece of toast and season with black pepper.

MOST PEOPLE THINK THAT THE HIGH-IN-FAT AND CALORIFIC AVOCADO WOULDN'T BE CONSIDERED GOOD FOR WEIGHT LOSS. RESEARCH IS NOW SUGGESTING THAT MONOUNSATURATED FATTY ACIDS, SUCH AS THOSE FOUND IN AVOCADOS, ARE LESS LIKELY TO BE STORED AS FAT AND MORE LIKELY TO BE USED AS ENERGY.

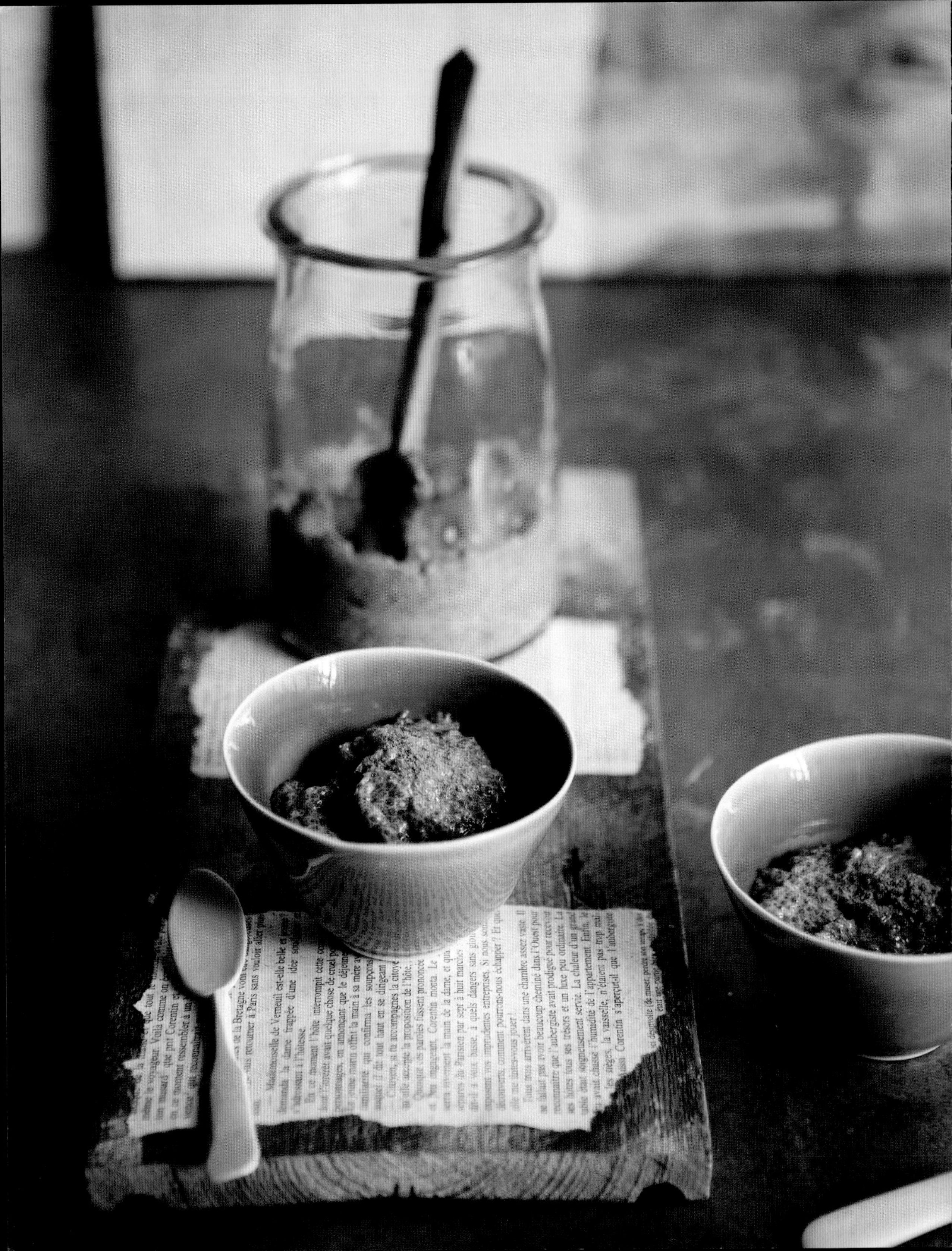

CHOCOLATE **CHIA** BREAKFAST PUDDING

360ml unsweetened almond milk
5 dates, pitted
½ teaspoon cacao powder
½ teaspoon ground cinnamon
Pinch of ground cloves
Pinch of ground nutmeg
Pinch of ground ginger
40g chia seeds

Serves 2

Chocolate for breakfast? Well, of course! It's allowed because in this recipe we are using the real deal, cacao. And cacao is jam-packed with antioxidants and a whole bunch of other good stuff for your body and mind. My youngest child, Nestor, is a chocoholic so when this very special breakfast pudding is on offer, he says I'm the best mummy in the whole wide world. Maybe I should make it more often!

Combine the almond milk, dates, cacao powder, cinnamon, cloves, nutmeg and ginger in a blender or food processor and blitz until smooth. Pour this into a mixing bowl and stir in the chia seeds.

Divide the mixture into 4 small bowls or Mason jars and place in the fridge for a few hours or overnight. This will allow the chia seeds to swell up to 10 times their size and make a delicious, jelly-like breakfast.

JUST A 28G SERVING OF CHIA SEEDS CONTAINS 18 PERCENT OF THE RECOMMENDED DAILY ALLOWANCE OF CALCIUM.

FAST-TRACK SAVERS

Combine four kids and their hectic schedules with my schedule and well, I admit it, I used to sometimes forget to eat and then wondered why I felt so sluggish during the day. So, a few years ago, I decided to create some uplifting treats in my kitchen that I could pack with me on those forgetful days. Most of them are jam-packed with one or two different superfoods, which, in my book, equates to a treasure trove of everything and anything good for my body.

So, if you've had an unhealthy lunch, skipped breakfast or have an indulgent dinner planned, these snacks, treats, juices and smoothies are just the thing to pick you up when your energy levels are flagging or you simply need to inject some concentrated goodness into your day.

You can either drink these immediately or pour them into a tight, sealable container to drink on-the-go when you need a healthy pick-me-up.

PARSLEY GREEN-GLOW SMOOTHIE

I spent a lot of time perfecting a smoothie that not only gives me loads of energy, but also makes my skin, hair and eyes glow! Thus, the Parsley Green-Glow was born.

Large handful of chard, spinach or kale
Small handful of fresh flat-leaf parsley
Small handful of rocket
½ banana
½ pear
½ papaya
180ml coconut water

Serves 1

Shove everything into a blender or food processor and whizz until smooth. Drink immediately or pour into your on-the-go container to enjoy later.

BLUEBERRY AND SPINACH SMOOTHIE

I use Mason jars for my smoothies on the go, as they have great lids to stop any leaking. This is one of my favourite smoothies because it contains bee pollen and baobab, which in turn equate to protein, enzymes and antioxidants.

120ml coconut milk (or any other plant-based milk)
90g frozen blueberries
½ banana (frozen is good, too)
Handful of spinach, chard or kale
1 date, pitted
1 tablespoon bee pollen
1 tablespoon baobab powder

Serves 1

Throw everything into a blender or food processor and give it a good whizz until smooth. Drink immediately or pour into your on-the-go container to enjoy later.

CARROT, PEAR AND GINGER JUICE

When I make this juice, I like to put the kale in the juicer first, before the other ingredients, as it helps to extract more kale goodness.

2 handfuls of kale (optional)
4 carrots
1 pear
½ lemon, peeled
2.5cm piece of fresh ginger

Juicer

Serves 1

Push all the ingredients through a juicer one at a time and enjoy.

MATCHA AND OAT TRUFFLES

100g ground almonds
130g oat flour (or grind your
own from rolled oats)
2 tablespoons raw honey
2 tablespoons coconut oil,
melted
50g macadamia nuts
4 teaspoons matcha (green
tea) powder

Makes about 16

I call these little guys my cup of coffee or my shot of espresso because they wake me up instantly and are SO much better for me than that latte, cappuccino or espresso. Eat these amazing truffles on the days following a bad night's sleep, or when you are falling asleep at your desk. They will jolt you back to life in a flash.

Put the ground almonds, oat flour, honey, melted coconut oil, macadamia nuts and only 2 teaspoons of the matcha powder in a mixing bowl and mix until you have a sticky, green dough. Roll the mixture into bite-sized balls.

Put the remaining matcha powder in a plastic bag and, one by one, drop each ball inside the bag and shake until thoroughly coated in matcha powder.

Store in an airtight container in the fridge for up to 1 week.

MATCHA IS A POWDERED GREEN TEA THAT CAN ACTUALLY RELAX YOU WHILE ALSO KEEPING YOU ALERT. THIS IS DUE TO THE AMINO ACID L – THEANINE FOUND IN THE LEAVES USED TO MAKE MATCHA.

These truffles are the REAL deal, an authentic, natural burst of energy.

CARROT-CAKE ENERGY BALLS WITH **GOJI** GOODNESS

30g goji berries
135g rolled oats
25g ground almonds
2 tablespoons chia seeds
60g hazelnut butter
4 tablespoons maple syrup
½ teaspoon vanilla extract
½ teaspoon ground cinnamon
¼ teaspoon ground ginger
¼ teaspoon ground nutmeg
65g grated carrots
30g oat flour (or grind your own from rolled oats)

Makes 12–16

My favourite cake, hands down, has always been carrot cake. Even as a young girl, I would choose that flavour for my birthday cake. I'm obsessed! So I wanted to create a smaller, healthier version that I could just pop in my mouth when exhaustion struck. Not only do these small-but-mighty bites taste incredible, but they also take me down memory lane and give me an instant body AND mind boost.

Begin by soaking the goji berries in a cup of water and set aside for about 10 minutes, then drain.

Combine the oats, ground almonds and chia seeds in a mixing bowl. Add the hazelnut butter, maple syrup, vanilla extract, ground cinnamon, ginger and nutmeg, grated carrots and the soaked goji berries and mix well.

Scoop the dough out a tablespoon at a time and use your hands to roll each one into bite-sized balls.

Store in an airtight container in the fridge for up to 1 week.

GRAM FOR GRAM, THE LITTLE **GOJI BERRY** HAS ABOUT 500 TIMES MORE VITAMIN C THAN AN ORANGE AND CONSIDERABLY MORE BETA-CAROTENE THAN CARROTS.

CHOCOLATE AND LUCUMA TRUFFLES

15 dates, pitted
60g cacao powder,
  plus 2 teaspoons for dusting
30g carob powder
20g lucuma powder
1 teaspoon vanilla extract
25g goji berries
4 tablespoons coconut oil,
  melted

Makes about 12

Seriously short on time, or know you have the world's busiest week ahead? Well these bad boys take less than 5 minutes to make and taste so chocolatey and naughty that you might think they're bad for you. NOT the case! Instead, these bite-sized, perfect-on-the-go truffles are truly worthy of their superhero superfood designation.

Blend the dates, cacao, carob, lucuma, vanilla extract, goji berries and melted coconut oil in a blender or food processor. Once mixed, roll into bite-sized balls.

Put the remaining 2 teaspoons cacao powder in a plastic bag and, one by one, drop each ball inside the bag and shake until thoroughly coated in cacao.

Store in an airtight container in the fridge for up to 1 week.

These can be frozen for up to 3 months and taken out to defrost for that crazy day or week ahead.

LUCUMA IS REFERRED TO AS THE 'GOLD OF THE INCAS'; THE INCAS PRIZED THE LUCUMA FRUIT AS A HEALTHY SOURCE OF SUGAR, AND IT'S ALSO FULL OF FIBRE, VITAMINS, MINERALS AND ANTIOXIDANTS.

NUTS AND BANANAS COVERED IN CINNAMON AND CACAO BUTTER

170g mixed nuts (such as brazil nuts, walnuts, almonds and cashews)
50g cacao butter
3 tablespoons cacao powder
2 tablespoons raw honey
2 bananas, cut into 2cm rounds
3–4 teaspoons ground cinnamon

Baking tray lined with parchment paper

Serves 2–3

These are slightly messy, but worth keeping in a container that you can have to hand at your office, or in your briefcase or handbag. You only need to devour a couple at a time to feel an instant boost. If you're making these for your kids, make sure to have plenty of napkins to wipe those cinnamon and chocolate fingers!

Preheat the oven to 150°C/Gas 2 and spread the nuts out on a baking tray. Toast in the preheated oven for 15–20 minutes. Remove from the oven and leave to cool completely.

Meanwhile, melt the cacao butter in a saucepan. Once melted, mix in the cacao powder and honey and stir until fully dissolved. Remove from the heat and transfer the sauce to a mixing bowl.

Dip the nuts and banana slices into the melted chocolate, a couple at a time. Place the chocolate-covered nuts and bananas on the prepared baking tray and place in the fridge for the chocolate to set.

Once set, put the cinnamon in a plastic bag, add the nuts and bananas, a few at a time, and gently shake until they are thoroughly coated in cinnamon.

Store in an airtight container in the fridge for up to 3 days, or freeze for up to 1 month.

CACAO BUTTER IS A GREAT INGREDIENT TO USE TO MAKE A HEALTHY AND DELICIOUS CHOCOLATE SAUCE IN MINUTES. IT'S ONE OF NATURE'S SUPERFOODS, WITH FANTASTIC ANTIOXIDANT PROPERTIES.

'CHEESY' KALE CRISPS WITH LIME

150g kale
2 tablespoons coconut oil, melted
1 teaspoon coconut palm sugar
1 teaspoon ground flaxseed
½ teaspoon sea salt
Juice of ½ lime
50g nutritional yeast

Serves 2

King kale is being hailed as the veggie lover's beef, as gram for gram, it has more iron than beef. But more than that, kale is low calorie, high in fibre and has zero fat. And kale isn't just for smoothies or salads any more… You CAN have your crisps and eat them too, albeit a much healthier version!

Preheat the oven to 180°C/Gas 4. Remove the stalks and thick veins from the kale and tear them into small pieces. Put the kale in a bowl and drizzle over the melted coconut oil. Mix well, then use your hands to massage the oil into the kale for a few minutes to tenderise the leaves.

Add the coconut palm sugar, flaxseed, sea salt, lime juice and nutritional yeast and mix well.

Transfer the kale to a large baking tray and bake in the preheated oven for 30 minutes or until golden and slightly crispy. Take out of the oven and loosen the kale with a spatula. Turn the oven off and stick the tray back in for another 20 minutes, which allows it to become even crispier.

My kale crisps usually get eaten straightaway but you can store them in an airtight container for up to 1 week.

NOT ONLY DO LIMES CONTAIN A HIGH AMOUNT OF VITAMIN C, THEY ALSO CONTAIN FLAVONOIDS THAT HELP TO PROTECT THE EYES FROM AGING AND FROM INFECTIONS.

BEET – THE – BLUES
RAINBOW JUICE

1 beetroot
1 cucumber
4 carrots
150g blueberries
2.5cm piece of fresh ginger

Juicer

Serves 2

Juices are practically like getting an injection of nutrients directly into your blood stream. Think of them as nature's liquid medicine, and the best you can give your body. They re-charge, revive and re-fuel you within minutes. I particularly like this colourful juice because it's almost as if you're drinking a rainbow of health.

With this juice, there is no need to peel away any skin. Simply cut the beetroot, cucumber and carrots into quarters and add all the ingredients to your juicer.

This juice is best when drunk immediately, however, if you want to drink it on the go, squeeze half a lemon into the bottom of your on-the-go container before adding the juice. This helps to slow down the oxidation process (i.e. during which nutrients are lost and the juice turns brown).

IF YOU NEED A STAMINA BOOST FOR YOUR NEXT GYM SESSION, BEETROOT HAS BEEN SHOWN TO IMPROVE ATHLETIC PERFORMANCE. THE JUICE CAN HELP YOUR MUSCLES WORK MORE EFFICIENTLY AND LOWER THE OXYGEN UPTAKE IN THE MUSCLES AS WELL.

POWER PROTEIN BARS
WITH HEMP

3 tablespoons chia seeds
135ml water
135g rolled oats
65g hazelnuts, chopped
65g walnuts, chopped
80g coconut oil
3 tablespoons raw honey
2 teaspoons vanilla extract
2 tablespoons cacao powder
2 teaspoons carob powder
175g dates, pitted and chopped
160g shelled hemp seeds

20cm square baking tin lined
   with parchment paper
   overlapping the sides

Makes about 12

If you really want more protein in your diet, but would rather not rely so much on animal protein, this power bar has been made especially for you. Believe it or not, we can get so much protein from plant-based sources. I know that when I was growing up, I actually thought protein only came from animals. As I later discovered, there is actually a plethora of protein in plants, so eat up!

Begin by soaking the chia seeds in the 135ml water in a bowl and put to one side. Preheat the oven to 150°C/Gas 2 and spread the rolled oats and chopped nuts out on a baking tray. Lightly toast in the preheated oven for 10–15 minutes, stirring every so often. Remove from the oven, leave to cool, then transfer to a mixing bowl.

Meanwhile, melt the coconut oil with the honey, vanilla extract, and cacao and carob powders in a small saucepan. Pour this over the oats and nuts and stir in the dates, hemp seeds and soaked chia seeds.

Increase the oven temperature to 180°C/Gas 4. Pour the power protein mixture into the prepared tin, press down firmly, then bake for 20 minutes or until golden. Remove from the oven and leave to cool in the tin.

Once cooled, lift the sides of the parchment paper to remove the bars from the tin and cut into squares or bars. Store in an airtight container in the fridge for up to 2 weeks.

THE PROTEIN AND FIBRE FOUND IN HEMP HELPS TO SLOW DOWN DIGESTION, WHICH IN TURN PREVENTS A BLOOD SUGAR SPIKE AND THEREFORE SUSTAINS OUR ENERGY FOR LONGER PERIODS.

DREAMY **FIG** AND SPIRULINA BITES

45g rolled oats
75g cashews
150g dried figs
2 tablespoons desiccated
  coconut
½ teaspoon vanilla extract
Grated zest of 1 lemon
4 tablespoons lemon juice
2 teaspoons spirulina powder
2 tablespoons tahini
2 tablespoons water

Makes 12–15

Oh algae, you are the new kid on the block. Well, actually you are one of the oldest life forms on the planet, but we've only recently discovered you are incredibly beneficial to our health. Spirulina is an algae powerhouse of nutrients unlike any grain, plant or fruit. That's why I love to incorporate it, not only in my smoothies, but also in these good-to-go bite-sized bursts of health.

Put the oats in a blender or food processor and blitz into fine crumbs. Add the remaining ingredients and blend until smooth.

Transfer the mixture to a mixing bowl and use your hands to roll into walnut-sized balls.

Store in an airtight container in the fridge for up to 2 weeks.

FIGS CONTAIN MORE CALCIUM THAN MOST OTHER FRUITS. IN FACT, ONE SERVING OF DRIED FIGS EQUALS 12 PERCENT OF YOUR RDA FOR CALCIUM.

SUPER–HEALTHY GRANOLA AND **CRANBERRY** BARS

350g dates, pitted
270g rolled oats
80g almonds
35g pumpkin seeds
60g dried cranberries
120ml maple syrup
120g hazelnut butter

20cm square baking tin lined with parchment paper

Makes about 10

Made in a flash, these bars will keep for several days so you will have a hearty, sustaining snack to see you through the week.

There are so many incredibly unhealthy granola bars out there that are seeping with refined sugar, and that's something I didn't want my kids eating or me either! These bars are quite a hearty snack and they will keep you full for hours and pack in a healthy amount of fibre, protein and omega 3s.

Put the dates, oats and almonds in a blender or food processor and blitz until only small bits remain. Transfer to a mixing bowl. Add the pumpkin seeds and cranberries and mix well.

Mix the maple syrup and hazelnut butter together in a small bowl. Drizzle it over the date mixture and mix well. I find using my hands works best as you want to get it to a thick dough. Transfer the dough to the prepared baking tin and press down until it is flat and has covered the entire tin. Place in the fridge for 20 minutes to set.

Remove the chilled slab from the tin and cut into about 10 squares or bars.

Store in an airtight container in the fridge for up to 1 week.

CRANBERRIES AREN'T JUST FOR CHRISTMAS AND THANKSGIVING! THESE SMALL BUT MIGHTY BERRIES ARE GREAT FOR THE HEALTH OF YOUR MOUTH. THEY CAN PREVENT BAD BACTERIA FROM DOING DAMAGE TO YOUR MOUTH AND TEETH.

PORTABLE LUNCHES

Just like with a lot of the breakfast recipes, a little planning goes a long way to feeling great throughout your day. If you're out and about and want to guarantee that you are eating 'the right stuff' for your lunch, then this chapter is for you! The recipes are simple to make, but you are guaranteed a shot of 'real' energy with every bite.

As a bonus, my definition of portable lunches expands to the word 'picnic'! It's so easy to whip up several of these recipes and bring them out on your picnic rug to really impress your guests.

SUSHI-STYLE SPINACH AND BEANSPROUT BOWL WITH A GINGER DRESSING

480ml water
190g brown rice
25g goji berries
100g shelled edamame
1 nori sheet
1 avocado, peeled, pitted and
  sliced
Large handful of spinach
Large handful of beansprouts
2 teaspoons sesame seeds
Dulse flakes, to serve

For the ginger dressing
60ml apple cider vinegar
2.5cm piece of fresh ginger,
  minced
1 date, pitted
1 tablespoon umeboshi paste
1 teaspoon tamari

Serves 2

This is basically veggie sushi but without having to put in the effort to create perfect rolls, which makes it much quicker to assemble.

Bring the 480ml water to the boil in a saucepan, then add the brown rice. Reduce the heat to low, cover and simmer for 45–60 minutes. Once cooked, rinse in cold water.

Soak the goji berries in water for 10 minutes, then drain.

Meanwhile, bring another saucepan of water to the boil, add the edamame and cook for 5 minutes, then drain and rinse in cold water. Chop the nori sheet into small pieces.

Divide the cooked rice between 2 bowls and top with the sliced avocado, edamame, soaked goji berries, and the spinach, beansprouts and sesame seeds.

To make the ginger dressing, put all the ingredients in a blender or food processor and blitz until smooth. Pour the dressing over the 2 bowls and garnish with a sprinkle of dulse flakes.

BEANSPROUTS, BELIEVE IT OR NOT, ARE A NUTRITIONAL POWERHOUSE: THEY ARE RICH IN VITAMIN C AND A GOOD SOURCE OF 6 OUT OF THE 8 B VITAMINS.

MOROCCAN CHICKPEA, CARROT AND DATE SALAD WITH **PAPRIKA** DRESSING

1 x 400g tin chickpeas, drained and rinsed
1 small red onion, chopped
2 small carrots, grated
2 large handfuls of spinach
6 dates, pitted and chopped

For the paprika dressing
2 tablespoons olive oil
1 tablespoon tamari
1 teaspoon ground cumin
1 teaspoon paprika
Juice of 1 lemon

Serves 2

Just like Morocco itself, this salad is incredibly colourful and the flavours really shine through. This is my go-to lunch when I'm feeling really run down, as it incorporates some veg, dark green leaves, protein from the chickpeas and a natural sweetener – dates – all marinated in a delicious spice dressing. **(See photograph on page 71.)**

Put the chickpeas, onion, carrots, spinach and dates in a large bowl and toss everything together.

Whisk all the dressing ingredients together in a small bowl.

Drizzle the dressing over the chickpea salad and leave to marinate for at least 1 hour.

Pour the dressing over the salad in the morning before work, and by lunchtime the salad will be perfectly marinated.

GRINDING DRIED RED PEPPERS INTO A FINE POWDER MAKES PAPRIKA. JUST 1 TABLESPOON PROVIDES AN AMPLE AMOUNT OF CAROTENOIDS (THUS ITS RICH RED COLOUR), THE FAMILY THAT INCLUDES VITAMIN A, WHICH IS GREAT FOR OUR EYESIGHT.

WILD RICE, BEETROOT AND GRAPE SALAD WITH A HONEY, MAPLE AND MUSTARD DRESSING

480ml water
130g wild rice
2 small (raw) beetroots
20 red grapes, halved
Large handful of fresh flat-leaf
   parsley, chopped
2 tablespoons sunflower seeds
2 spring onions, chopped

**For the honey, maple and
   mustard dressing**
1 tablespoon olive oil
½ tablespoon apple cider
   vinegar
½ teaspoon maple syrup
½ teaspoon raw honey
½ teaspoon English mustard
1 tablespoon fresh lemon juice
Sea salt and freshly ground
   black pepper

Serves 2

Wild rice is gluten free and is brimming with antioxidants – about 30 times more than white rice. Although it takes about an hour to cook, it's worth it, as this rice has a delicious nutty flavour. **(See photograph on page 70.)**

Put the 480ml water in a saucepan and bring it to the boil. Add the wild rice, reduce the heat to low, cover and simmer for 1 hour.

Meanwhile, peel the raw beetroots and slice them into very thin rounds. Once the rice is cooked, drain off any remaining water and leave the rice to cool.

Put the cooked rice in a large bowl and add the sliced beetroot, red grapes, parsley, sunflower seeds and spring onions.

Whisk all the dressing ingredients, plus a pinch of salt and pepper, together in a bowl, then pour over the rice salad. Toss everything together before serving.

BEETROOT CONTAINS NATURALLY OCCURRING NITRATES, WHICH THE BODY CONVERTS INTO NITRIC OXIDE. THIS HELPS TO RELAX YOUR BLOOD VESSELS, WHICH IN TURN IMPROVES BLOOD FLOW AND HELPS TO LOWER BLOOD PRESSURE.

SQUASH, MUSHROOM AND KALE SALAD WITH PUMPKIN AND POMEGRANATE

1 small butternut squash, peeled, deseeded and diced
3 tablespoons coconut oil, melted
2 teaspoons ground cumin
1 shallot, chopped
200g portabellini mushrooms, thinly sliced
Bunch of kale
3 tablespoons pumpkin seeds
Seeds from 1 pomegranate
2 tablespoons olive oil
1 tablespoon apple cider vinegar
Sea salt and freshly ground black pepper

Serves 4

Kale may not be the first thing that comes to mind when you think of a salad. However, the trick to using kale in your salads and making it so tasty is to massage the leaves. It takes no time at all and it's definitely worth it!

Preheat the oven to 180°C/Gas 4. Put the squash in a bowl with 2 tablespoons of the melted coconut oil and the cumin and season with salt and pepper. Mix well, then transfer to a roasting tin and bake in the preheated oven for about 40 minutes, flipping every 15 minutes. Once cooked, remove from the oven and leave to cool.

Meanwhile, coat a frying pan with the remaining coconut oil and set over a medium to high heat. Add the chopped shallot and mushrooms and season with salt and pepper. Gently fry for 10 minutes, or until soft, then put to one side.

Remove the stalks from the kale, stack the leaves on top of each other and roll up like a cigar shape, then slice into ribbons. Put the kale in a large bowl with 1 teaspoon sea salt and massage the leaves with your hands for 3–5 minutes. You will begin to see the kale soften as the moisture starts to seep out. Add the roasted squash, fried mushrooms and shallot and the pumpkin seeds and pomegranate seeds. Drizzle over the olive oil and apple cider vinegar before serving.

HIGH IN FIBRE, VITAMINS AND PHYTOCHEMICALS, POMEGRANATE IS MAGICAL! PERFECT IN BREAKFAST CEREALS, SALADS AND SOUPS – GET POMEGRANATE SEEDS IN YOUR DIET WHENEVER YOU CAN.

This salad works just as well as a
side dish as it does as a portable lunch.

MARINATED TOFU WITH AN ALMOND–BUTTER SAUCE, WRAPPED IN WHOLEWHEAT TORTILLAS

450g firm tofu
2 wholewheat tortillas
1 carrot, grated
¼ cucumber, grated
2 leaves of romaine lettuce, shredded
½ red onion, thinly sliced
Handful of fresh coriander, chopped
Sesame seeds, for sprinkling

For the marinade
4 tablespoons olive oil
2 garlic cloves, crushed
2 tablespoons tamari
1 tablespoon maple syrup
1 teaspoon dried chilli flakes

For the almond-butter sauce
2 tablespoons almond butter
½ tablespoon raw honey
½ tablespoon tamari
1 tablespoon olive oil

Serves 2

I've created this recipe with tofu, but you can easily swap the tofu for prawns and still use the same sweet and spicy marinade.

Pat the tofu dry with some kitchen roll. Line a plate with some kitchen roll and place the tofu on top. Place another small plate on top of the tofu and weight it down with something heavy (a tin of beans always works for me). Leave for about 15 minutes for the excess water to seep out of the tofu.

Meanwhile, whisk all the marinade ingredients together in a small bowl.

Slice the pressed tofu into strips, toss the strips in the marinade until coated, then transfer to the fridge to marinate for at least 30 minutes. Mix the almond-butter sauce ingredients together in a small bowl.

Once marinated, divide the tofu strips between the tortillas, placing them in the centre and drizzle with some of the sauce. Top with the carrots, cucumber, romaine lettuce, red onion and coriander. Drizzle a bit more of the sauce over and sprinkle with sesame seeds. Roll up each tortilla into a wrap, wrap tightly in foil or clingfilm, pop in a container and you are good to go!

WHOLEWHEAT TORTILLAS ARE NUTRITIONALLY SUPERIOR TO THE MORE COMMON WHITE–FLOUR VARIETY, AS PRODUCTS MADE FROM WHITE FLOUR HAVE BEEN STRIPPED OF PRETTY MUCH ALL THEIR ESSENTIAL NUTRIENTS.

SWEET POTATO AND PARSLEY FALAFEL CABBAGE WRAPS

200g sweet potatoes
Small handful of fresh flat-leaf
  parsley
Small handful of fresh
  coriander
75g walnuts
1 garlic clove
½ onion, chopped
1½ tablespoons coconut oil
½ teaspoon ground cumin
½ tablespoon wholegrain flour
  (e.g. buckwheat, spelt or oat)
5–6 cabbage leaves

For the dairy-free cream
125ml coconut or soy yogurt
½ small cucumber, peeled,
  deseeded and shredded
Small handful of fresh mint,
  leaves only, finely chopped
½ teaspoon dried chilli flakes
1 garlic clove, crushed
½ teaspoon ground cumin

For the salsa
125g cherry tomatoes, diced
¼ red chilli, deseeded and
  finely chopped
½ garlic clove, crushed
Small handful of fresh
  coriander, chopped
½ tablespoon olive oil
Sea salt and freshly ground
  black pepper

Baking tray lined with
  parchment paper

Makes 5–6 wraps

I love sweet potatoes, so I've been looking for interesting ways to cook them. This recipe combines sweet potato with a great dairy-free topping and an extra spicy salsa. I used a cabbage leaf to wrap the falafels in, but you can use whatever leaves you have in the fridge.

Preheat the oven to 200°C/Gas 6 and prick the sweet potatoes a few times with a fork. Bake in the preheated oven for about 30 minutes or until soft. Leave to cool completely, then scoop the flesh into a large bowl. Leave the oven on to bake the falafel.

To make the dairy-free cream, put all the ingredients in a bowl, mix well and stick in the fridge for about 30 minutes. To make the salsa, mix all the ingredients together in a bowl.

For the falafels, blend the parsley, coriander and walnuts in a food processor until combined, then slowly add the garlic, onion, coconut oil, cumin, flour and sweet potato flesh, blending until the mixture becomes like a paste. Use your hands to roll the mixture into 10–12 small falafels and place them on the prepared baking tray. Bake for 20 minutes, turning every 5 minutes, or until they are a lovely brown colour.

Top each cabbage leaf with 2 falafels. Spoon some dairy-free cream and salsa on top, wrap it all up and take a big bite!

PARSLEY CONTAINS AN ARSENAL OF ANTIOXIDANTS AND INCLUDES A PARTICULAR FLAVONOID, LUTEOLIN, THAT HELPS TO ERADICATE FREE RADICALS.

BEETROOT, BLACK RICE AND PEAR WRAPS

4 wholewheat tortillas
2 large romaine lettuce leaves, torn in half
1 large pear, grated
Sea salt

For the beetroot paste
2 cooked beetroots, roughly chopped
1 garlic clove, crushed
Small handful of fresh coriander
Small handful of fresh flat-leaf parsley
35g walnuts
1 teaspoon coconut oil
2 teaspoons apple cider vinegar

For the black rice
240ml water
100g black rice
½ teaspoon caraway seeds
Finely grated zest and juice of ½ lime
35g sultanas
35g flaked almonds, toasted

Makes 4

I especially love this recipe because not only is it tasty in every way possible, but also it's a big hit with my children. It's incredibly easy to 'hide' really amazing foods that your children might not normally eat – and here's how!

To make the beetroot paste, throw everything into a food processor, add a pinch of sea salt to taste, and blitz until a lovely paste has formed. Transfer to a bowl for later.

To make the black rice, put the 240ml water in a saucepan and bring to the boil. Add the rice, caraway seeds and a pinch of sea salt. Reduce the heat to low, cover and leave to simmer for 20–25 minutes, or until all the water is absorbed, then leave to cool. Once cooled, transfer the rice to a bowl and add the lime zest and juice, sultanas and almonds. Stir well.

Place 2 tablespoons of the beetroot paste in the middle of each tortilla and cover with one of the lettuce leaf halves. Top with a couple of heaped spoonfuls of the black rice filling. Sprinkle with the grated pear and fold or roll the tortillas to create a wrap.

BROWN RICE IS GOOD FOR YOU, BUT **BLACK RICE** IS EVEN BETTER. IT MAY TAKE LONGER TO COOK, BUT IF YOU HAVE THE TIME THEN GO FOR IT. THE BRAN HULL IN BLACK RICE CONTAINS SIGNIFICANTLY HIGHER AMOUNTS OF VITAMIN E, WHICH HELPS TO PROTECT THE CELLS FROM THOSE FREE RADICALS.

Banish boring sandwiches and make a batch of these tasty wraps for the whole family.

ROASTED CHICKPEA AND SUN-DRIED TOMATO SALAD WITH HERB DRESSING

1 x 400g tin chickpeas, drained
and rinsed
1 tablespoon olive oil
½ teaspoon ground cumin
¼ teaspoon paprika
¼ teaspoon ground turmeric
Large handful of fresh flat-leaf
parsley, chopped
35g pine nuts
25g sun-dried tomatoes, thinly
sliced
2 spring onions, chopped
90g black olives
Sea salt and freshly ground
black pepper

For the herb dressing
2 tablespoons olive oil
1 garlic clove
Juice of 1 lemon
1 tablespoon apple cider
vinegar
1 tablespoon maple syrup
Small handful of fresh
coriander
Small handful of fresh mint

Baking tray lined with
aluminium foil

Serves 2

Not only is this recipe chock-full of greens for your health, but the flavour really shines through, too. I use sun-dried tomatoes a lot when I cook because of their amazing flavour. Luckily, even after being dried in the sun, they still keep their nutritional value – they are just losing most of their water content. You don't have to add a lot of these to your recipes to get that burst of flavour; just a few will do.

Preheat the oven to 180°C/Gas 4.

Combine the chickpeas, olive oil, cumin, paprika and turmeric in a bowl. Season to taste with salt and pepper. Spread the chickpea mixture out over the the prepared baking tray. Place the tray on the upper rack of the preheated oven and roast for about 1 hour. Remove from the oven and leave to cool.

To make the herb dressing, put all the ingredients in a blender or food processor and whizz until mixed.

Combine the parsley, pine nuts, sun-dried tomatoes, spring onions, black olives and the cooled chickpeas in a salad bowl. Drizzle over the herb dressing and toss everything together before serving.

CHICKPEAS ARE SUPER-HIGH IN FIBRE AND PROTEIN, PLUS THEY ARE LOW ON THE GLYCEMIC INDEX, WHICH MEANS THESE LITTLE BEANS CAN REALLY HELP KEEP YOU FEELING FULLER FOR LONGER. CHICKPEAS ALSO CONTAIN A HEALTHY DOES OF PHOSPHORUS, WHICH IS A KEY PLAYER IN BONE HEALTH.

GREEN GODDESS SALAD WITH BLOOD-ORANGE DRESSING

1 head of lettuce (the darker in colour the better), leaves separated
1 small cucumber, chopped
3 vine tomatoes, chopped
2 spring onions, chopped
Large handful of black olives
1 red onion, sliced
1 avocado, peeled, pitted and diced
20g pine nuts, toasted

For the blood-orange dressing
Juice of ½ blood orange
120ml apple cider vinegar
2 tablespoons tamari
Handful of fresh coriander
Handful of fresh flat-leaf parsley
Handful of fresh mint
1 small garlic clove
1 tablespoon raw honey or 1 date, pitted
Sea salt and freshly ground black pepper

Serves 2

I've been making this salad for nearly two years now. It is so nutritious and tasty that even after having it at least once a week, I still love it. Part of the reason it is so delicious is thanks to its yummy dressing. You may never have thought of putting avocado in a dressing before, but it makes it lovely and creamy (and it's a perfectly effortless way to get your children to eat their greens).

Combine the lettuce leaves, cucumber, tomatoes, spring onions, olives, red onion, half the avocado and the pine nuts in a large salad bowl.

Put all the dressing ingredients in a blender or food processor with the remaining avocado and blitz until smooth. This is a thick dressing, so if you'd like it thinner, add 1–2 tablespoons water. Season to taste with salt and pepper.

Smother your salad with the dressing and watch it be devoured.

NOT ONLY DO **BLOOD ORANGES** HAVE THE BENEFIT OF A HUGE AMOUNT OF VITAMIN C, THEY ALSO CONTAIN ANTHOCYANINS, ANTIOXIDANTS FOUND IN BERRIES AND RED WINE.

PUY LENTIL, ARTICHOKE AND SUN-DRIED TOMATO SALAD WITH RASPBERRY DRESSING

1.2 litres water
200g Puy lentils
2 large handfuls of kale, torn into bite-sized pieces
1 small red onion, finely chopped
25g sun-dried tomatoes, roughly chopped
1 x 400g tin artichoke hearts in water, drained and chopped

For the raspberry dressing
50g raspberries
1 teaspoon lemon juice
2 teaspoons apple cider vinegar
2 tablespoons maple syrup
1 tablespoon olive oil
2 tablespoons water

Serves 2

This is a good combo of fruit, veggie and legumes in one salad, and therefore a good all-round nutrition hit. It's quick and easy to put together, ensuring this salad will keep you coming back for more. **(See photograph on page 71.)**

Put 480ml of the water in a saucepan, bring to the boil, then add the lentils. Bring back to the boil, then simmer for 10–15 minutes until all of the water has been absorbed, stirring every now and then. Once cooked, rinse the lentils under cool water and transfer to a large bowl.

Meanwhile, put the remaining 720ml water in a separate saucepan, bring to the boil and add the kale. Cook for 5 minutes, then drain, rinse with cool water and add to the lentils, along with the red onion, sun-dried tomatoes and artichokes.

Put all the dressing ingredients in a blender or food processor and blitz until smooth and combined.

Your lovely salad is now ready to be served! Drizzle the dressing over the lentil salad, toss everything together and you are ready to tuck in right away or transfer to a portable container and take it to go.

EATING ARTICHOKES HAS SHOWN TO HELP WITH DIGESTIVE ISSUES, SUCH AS AN IRRITABLE STOMACH OR BOWEL.

RADISH AND AVOCADO SALAD WITH CHIA TAHINI DRESSING

About 24 radishes, roughly
  chopped
2 small red peppers, deseeded
  and chopped
Large handful of black or
  kalamata olives
Large handful of fresh
  coriander, roughly chopped
1 small avocado, peeled, pitted
  and diced
½ red onion, thinly sliced
1 spring onion, chopped

For the chia tahini dressing
2 tablespoons chia seeds
2 tablespoons tahini
½ tablespoon cumin seeds
Juice of 1 lemon
1 tablespoon chopped fresh
  flat-leaf parsley
½ teaspoon tamari
1 tablespoon raw honey
Pinch of sea salt
Pinch of chilli powder

Serves 2–4

Radishes may not be your first choice to put into your lunch, but trust me – they're worth it. People think that they're not the tastiest of vegetables, but combine them with a killer salad dressing like the one in this recipe and you're in for a nutritious burst of a treat.

Put all the salad ingredients in a large salad or serving bowl.

Put all the dressing ingredients in a blender or food processor and blitz until smooth. The dressing will be quite thick but as you mix it through the salad, it will coat the ingredients nicely.

Pour the dressing over the salad, toss together until well combined and serve.

START PAYING MORE ATTENTION TO RADISHES. NOT ONLY DO 4 RADISHES MAKE UP ABOUT 14 PERCENT OF THE RDA OF VITAMIN C, BUT RESEARCH HAS ALSO SHOWN THAT THE ANTIOXIDANTS FOUND IN THEM MAY HELP PREVENT CANCER.

If you're not a tofu fan, replace it with pieces of marinated chicken.

BAKED TOFU AND APPLE ON MIXED GREENS AND WAKAME

450g firm tofu
1 tablespoon olive oil
1 tablespoon tamari
1 tablespoon apple cider
  vinegar
1 tablespoon lemon juice
10g dried wakame
100g mixed salad greens
1 apple, cored and thinly sliced
2 spring onions, chopped
2 tablespoons sesame seeds
1 tablespoon olive oil
1 teaspoon dried chilli flakes

Baking tray lined with
  parchment paper

Serves 2

This is a dish that even my kids honestly, whole-heartedly love. Adding flavour to foods like tofu, which start out quite bland, really helps to spice things up. With minimum effort, you can turn a simple mixed green salad into something super.

Pat the tofu dry with some kitchen roll. Line a plate with some kitchen roll and place the tofu on top. Place another small plate on top of the tofu and weight it down with something heavy (a tin of beans always works for me). Leave for 15–30 minutes for the liquid to seep out. Remove the plate and cut the pressed tofu into cubes. Mix the olive oil, tamari, apple cider vinegar and lemon juice together in a small bowl. Pour this over the tofu and leave it to marinate for 30 minutes. Preheat the oven to 180°C/Gas 4.

Arrange the tofu on the prepared baking tray in a single layer. Depending on how large your cubes are, bake the tofu in the preheated oven for 25–40 minutes until golden.

Meanwhile, soak the dried wakame in tepid water for 10–20 minutes. Pat dry with a tea towel or kitchen roll and coarsely chop. Put the salad greens, apple, spring onions, sesame seeds and wakame in a large bowl and toss with the olive oil and chilli flakes. Top with the baked tofu and serve.

MANY OF US ARE PROBABLY LACKING IN IODINE AND THAT'S EXACTLY WHAT WAKAME IS A GOOD SOURCE OF. IODINE IS NEEDED TO HELP CONVERT FOOD INTO ENERGY, BUT ALSO HELPS TO KEEP THE THYROID GLAND IN BALANCE.

LEMON SWEET POTATO SALAD WITH EDAMAME AND SUNFLOWER SEEDS

250g sweet potatoes
125g shelled edamame
45g sunflower seeds
Small handful of fresh mint, chopped

For the lemon dressing
2 tablespoons olive oil
1 tablespoon lemon juice
Grated zest of ½ lemon
Small garlic clove, crushed
1 tablespoon maple syrup

Serves 2

Sweet potatoes have become a real staple in our house and definitely trump the white ones. From sweet potato chips to soups and even in puddings, the sweet potato is a superstar when it comes to creating interesting and tasty recipes. Everyone loves a potato salad, but this one could knock socks off at your next picnic. And why wait for a picnic to enjoy a potato salad? A hearty and healthy lunch is what you will get with this recipe!

Cut the sweet potato into chunks (keep the skins on, they're good for you!) Bring a saucepan of water to the boil and add the potatoes. Cook for 15–20 minutes, or until tender, then drain and set aside to cool.

Meanwhile, bring a pan of water to the boil, add the edamame and cook for 5 minutes. Drain and rinse.

Once the sweet potatoes are cool, put them in a large bowl and add the edamame, sunflower seeds and chopped mint.

Mix all the dressing ingredients together in a bowl, then drizzle over the sweet potato salad and serve.

TRY TO ALWAYS KEEP THE SKINS ON SWEET POTATOES AS THAT'S WHERE MUCH OF THEIR GOODNESS IS FOUND, SUCH AS VITAMIN C, VITAMIN A AND CALCIUM.

LENTIL AND COUSCOUS SALAD WITH ALMONDS AND ASPARAGUS

50g brown lentils
180ml water
50g Israeli couscous
8 asparagus spears
1 small red onion, sliced
45g capers
45g sultanas
2 large handfuls of watercress
40g almonds
16 cherry tomatoes, halved

For the vinaigrette

3 tablespoons olive oil
2 tablespoons apple cider
  vinegar
1 tablespoon lemon juice

Serves 2

This is an all-round great meal, especially when asparagus is in season. Salads nowadays have such a broad definition. Whereas they used to mean lettuce leaves topped with some dressing, I find I can just throw some good, wholesome legumes, nuts and veggies together and, for me, that is a mighty super salad. Here's one of them.

Put the lentils and 180ml water in a saucepan over a medium heat, bring to the boil, then reduce to a simmer for 20–25 minutes until cooked. If needed, drain the lentils, then run them under cool water. Transfer to a large bowl.

Meanwhile, put the couscous in a saucepan and cover with water. Bring to the boil, reduce to a simmer and cook for 5–8 minutes until it is tender. Remove from the heat, drain and rinse under cool water. Add the couscous to the lentils.

Fill a small saucepan halfway with water. Bring to the boil, then add the asparagus. Cook for 2–3 minutes only, then drain and rinse under cold water. Cut the asparagus into 3cm lengths and add to the lentils and couscous.

Add the red onion, capers, sultanas, watercress, almonds and cherry tomatoes to the bowl. Whisk the vinaigrette ingredients together in a small bowl and drizzle over the salad. Toss together and serve.

ASPARAGUS IS PARTICULARLY HIGH IN A DETOXIFYING COMPOUND CALLED GLUTATHIONE WHICH HELPS BREAK DOWN FREE RADICALS AND CARCINOGENS IN THE BODY.

CAULIFLOWER, GOJI BERRY AND ALMOND SALAD WITH TURMERIC DRESSING

35g goji berries
1 cauliflower, cut into
  small florets
2 tablespoons coconut oil,
  melted
2 small red onions, sliced
35g flaked almonds
Sea salt and freshly ground
  black pepper

For the turmeric dressing
4 tablespoons apple cider
  vinegar
Finely grated zest and juice
  of 2 lemons
1 garlic clove, crushed
¼ large, ripe avocado, peeled
  and pitted
1 tablespoon ground turmeric
1 tablespoon raw honey
Pinch of sea salt

Serves 2

As bizarre as this dish sounds, it is unbelievably good and possibly one of my favourites! I urge you to make it as soon as possible. The dressing is super-versatile and can be used to drizzle over a load of steamed or roasted vegetables as well.

Put the goji berries in a bowl of water and set aside to soak for 10 minutes. Preheat the oven to 180°C/Gas 4.

Toss the cauliflower in the coconut oil – really rub the oil into it. Season with salt and black pepper, place on a baking tray and roast in the preheated oven for 15 minutes. Remove the tray from the oven, add the sliced red onions and roast for another 15–20 minutes until tender. Transfer the roasted vegetables to a large bowl.

Toast the flaked almonds on a baking tray in the hot oven for 3–5 minutes. Drain the goji berries and add to the roasted veggies, along with the toasted almonds.

Combine all the dressing ingredients in a blender or food processor and blitz until you get a bright orange dressing. It's wonderful to look at and taste. Serve the salad with the dressing and devour!

TURMERIC IS A NATURAL AND POTENT ANTI-INFLAMMATORY THAT HAS BEEN SHOWN TO WORK JUST AS WELL AS MANY ANTI-INFLAMMATORY DRUGS, BUT WITHOUT THE SIDE EFFECTS. STUDIES ARE EVEN SUGGESTING THAT TURMERIC COULD SLOW THE PROGRESSION OF ALZHEIMER'S DISEASE BY REMOVING AMYLOID PLAQUE BUILD-UP IN THE BRAIN.

Believe it or not, this recipe is entirely raw,
and it's a super-fun way to eat courgettes!

COURGETTI SPAGHETTI WITH A SUN-DRIED TOMATO, BASIL AND AVOCADO SAUCE

1 red pepper, deseeded and
  sliced
3½ tablespoons apple cider
  vinegar
3½ tablespoons tamari
2 large courgettes

**For the sun-dried tomato, basil
and avocado sauce**
100g sun-dried tomatoes,
  soaked
½ avocado, peeled, pitted and
  chopped
60g pine nuts
5 fresh basil leaves
1 garlic clove
2 tablespoons olive oil
Grated zest and juice of
  1 lemon
Sea salt and freshly ground
  black pepper

Serves 2–3

Having a raw meal once a day is a fantastic way to give your body a rest and allow it to simply absorb all of the goodness from the ingredients. When we cook food, we lose quite a lot of the nutrients that we want to be consuming. This dish is a brilliant entry into raw food! First and foremost, if you don't have a spiraliser, don't worry! You can easily use a mandolin or julienne slicer instead.

Put the sliced red peppers in a bowl and add the tamari and apple cider vinegar. Cover and set aside to marinate.

Grab your spiraliser, mandolin or julienne slicer and get to work on the courgettes. Your aim is to create spaghetti- or tagliatelle-like strips. Put your strips into a bowl ready for the sauce.

Put all the sauce ingredients in a food processor and whizz away. You will get a paste-like sauce, but if it's too thick for you, simply add a bit of water to thin it out.

Pour the sauce over the courgetti, mix well, top with the marinated peppers and serve.

COURGETTES ARE EXTREMELY LOW IN CALORIES - ABOUT 19 CALORIES PER 120G - AND ARE MOSTLY WATER, WHICH MAKES THEM A DIETER'S FRIEND.

MAINS

I've been told before that 'supper' actually
means 'supplemental'... i.e. we are not supposed
to eat huge meals before bed, just a small,
supplemental amount. That way, our bodies
can rest and digest something manageable
while we're sleeping and when we wake, we
are recharged and ready to nourish our bodies
with a healthy and hearty breakfast. When we
eat something heavy in the evenings, it affects
our sleep and we wake up feeling lethargic. The
main dishes that I've created are light but filling,
so you don't go to bed feeling hungry, and you
wake up in the morning feeling great.

AUBERGINE, TOMATO AND ALMOND PASTA WITH QUINOA LEMON 'MEATBALLS'

2 large aubergines
2 tablespoons coconut oil, melted
200g almonds, soaked in water for 3–4 hours (optional)
100g sun-dried tomatoes, drained (or, if not from a jar, soak in water for 10 minutes and drain)
Large handful of fresh flat-leaf parsley
90g black olives, pitted
100ml olive oil
1 tablespoon raw honey
500g wholegrain pasta
Sea salt

For the 'meatballs'
240ml water
170g quinoa
1 tablespoon coconut oil
½ onion, finely chopped,
150g chestnut mushrooms, finely chopped
Small handful of fresh flat-leaf parsley, finely chopped
Small handful of fresh basil, finely chopped
Small handful of fresh coriander, finely chopped
1 teaspoon dried chilli flakes
Grated zest and juice of 2 lemons
2 tablespoons nutritional yeast
6 tablespoons oat flour (or any other wholewheat flour)
2 tablespoons olive oil

Serves 4–6

A healthier version of classic spaghetti with meatballs, this dish is still packed with protein, but it skips the saturated fat and cholesterol.

Preheat the oven to 180°C/Gas 4. Slice the aubergines into 1cm-thick rounds and place on a baking tray. Coat the aubergine with the coconut oil and a good sprinkling of sea salt. Roast in the preheated oven for 30–35 minutes, or until soft and golden. Leave to cool, then put the roasted aubergine, soaked almonds, sun-dried tomatoes, parsley, olives, olive oil and honey in a food processor and blitz to a lovely paste.

For the 'meatballs', put the 240ml water in a saucepan and bring to the boil. Add the quinoa, bring back to the boil, cover and simmer for about 20 minutes until cooked. Leave to cool. Preheat the oven again to 180°C/Gas 4 if it isn't still on.

Heat the coconut oil in a frying pan over a medium heat. Add the onion and mushrooms and cook for 5–7 minutes, or until the onion is translucent and soft. Transfer to a bowl with the cooled quinoa and the rest of the 'meatball' ingredients. Mix well, then shape into golf ball-sized 'meatballs'. Place on a baking tray and bake in the hot oven for 30 minutes, or until browned, flipping halfway through. Leave to cool.

Cook the pasta according to the packet instructions, until al dente. Drain and divide between bowls. Pour over the pesto, mix well and top with the 'meatballs'.

AUBERGINES ARE RICH IN ANTIOXIDANTS, PARTICULARLY NASUNIN, WHICH IS PREDOMINANTLY FOUND IN THE SKIN OF AUBERGINES – SO DON'T PEEL IT OFF!

Herb-packed quinoa 'meatballs' with spaghetti and an aubergine pesto make for a totally new and utterly delicious dinner.

BUTTERNUT BARLEY STEW
WITH CAVOLO NERO

1 tablespoon coconut oil
1 onion, finely chopped
2 small red chillies, deseeded
   and chopped
2 garlic cloves, crushed
1 teaspoon ground cumin
200g pearl barley
1 butternut squash, peeled and
   cut into chunks
1 litre vegetable stock
1 x 400g tin cannellini beans,
   drained and rinsed
2 large handfuls of cavolo nero,
   torn into small pieces
Small handful of fresh flat-leaf
   parsley, chopped
Sea salt and freshly ground
   black pepper

Serves 4

Every now and again, you need some warming, comforting food. Unfortunately, 'comfort' food isn't always very healthy or nutritious! So, I've created my own comforting stew that's full of good stuff, making you feel nourished both inside and out.

Heat the coconut oil in a large frying pan over a medium heat and fry the onion for 5–7 minutes until soft. Add the red chillies, garlic and cumin and fry for another 1–2 minutes.

Add the pearl barley, butternut squash and the vegetable stock. Bring to the boil, then reduce the heat to low and simmer for about 45 minutes. Add the cannellini beans and cavolo nero for the last 5 minutes, making sure the cavolo nero is soft before you serve.

Serve in soup bowls and top with the chopped parsley and some salt and black pepper.

CAVOLO NERO, ALSO KNOWS AS TUSCAN BLACK KALE, IS AMONG THE MOST ANTIOXIDANT–RICH FOODS ON EARTH.

RED PEPPERS STUFFED WITH BULGHUR WHEAT AND PISTACHIOS

8 red peppers
3 tablespoons coconut oil, melted
500ml vegetable stock
250g bulghur wheat
1 onion, finely chopped
1 teaspoon ground cumin
2 garlic cloves, crushed
3 portobello mushrooms
100g cherry tomatoes, cut into quarters
2 carrots, grated
2 large handfuls of spinach
100g pistachio nuts, roughly chopped

Serves 8

I like all the colours in this dish – the more colours, the more antioxidants, and therefore the more nutritious for you. And this one's a great option when you're entertaining friends, too!

Preheat the oven to 180°C/Gas 4. Cut the tops off the peppers, scoop out the seeds and place the peppers in a roasting tin. Brush them lightly with 1 tablespoon of the coconut oil and bake in the preheated oven for 20 minutes, or until lightly browned. Leave to cool, but leave the oven on.

Bring the vegetable stock to the boil in a saucepan and add the bulghur wheat. Reduce the heat to a simmer, cover and cook for 15–20 minutes. Meanwhile, melt the remaining coconut oil in a large frying pan and fry the onion for 5–7 minutes until translucent. Add the cumin and garlic and continue to fry for 2 more minutes. Add the mushrooms and cook for a further 10–15 minutes, or until soft.

Once the bulghur wheat is cooked and has absorbed all the stock, add it to the frying pan, along with the tomatoes, grated carrot and spinach, and cook for another 2–3 minutes, stirring, until the spinach is soft.

Fill the peppers with the bulghur mixture, then place them back in the roasting tin, standing up. Bake for a further 10 minutes, then remove from the oven and season with salt and black pepper. Top with the chopped pistachios before serving.

PISTACHIOS CONTAIN PHYTOCHEMICALS AND OTHER ANTIOXIDANTS, SUCH AS VITAMIN E AND SELENIUM WHICH HELP TO DESTROY TISSUE – DAMAGING FREE RADICALS WITHIN THE BODY.

BEETROOT, QUINOA, BLACK BEAN AND FLAXSEED BURGERS

180ml water
90g quinoa
200g tinned black beans, drained and rinsed
2 cooked beetroots
1 shallot, finely chopped
2 garlic cloves, crushed
Small handful of fresh coriander, chopped
2 tablespoons apple cider vinegar
Juice of 1 lime
2 tablespoons oat flour (or grind your own from rolled oats)
2 tablespoons ground flaxseed
2 tablespoons coconut oil
Sea salt and freshly ground black pepper

To serve
6 wholewheat buns, toasted
Tahini
Dried chilli flakes, to season
2 avocados, peeled, pitted and sliced (optional)

Serves 6

Think your regular all-beef burger has a lot of protein in it? Well, this veggie alternative is a serious contender not only from the beans, but from the quinoa, too. And the colour from the beetroot makes it a feast for the eyes!

Put the 180ml water and quinoa in a saucepan, bring to the boil, then reduce the heat to low and simmer for 15–20 minutes, or until all the water has been absorbed and the quinoa is tender. Leave to cool.

Once the quinoa has cooled, put it in a food processor and add the black beans, beetroots, shallot, garlic, coriander, apple cider vinegar and lime juice. Blitz until smooth. Transfer the mixture to a large bowl and stir in the oat flour and flaxseed. Season to taste. Divide the mixture into 6 equal portions and flatten into fat discs to create your burgers.

Melt the coconut oil in a frying pan over a medium to high heat. Cook each burger for 2–3 minutes on each side.

Serve on toasted wholewheat buns spread with tahini and sprinkled with chilli flakes. Add sliced avocado for a real treat.

FLAXSEED GIVES YOU A DOUBLE-WHAMMY OF FIBRE BECAUSE IT CONTAINS BOTH INSOLUBLE AND SOLUBLE FIBRE.

BROCCOLI AND SHIITAKE SOBA NOODLE BOWL

250g soba noodles
250g Tenderstem broccoli
2 tablespoons coconut oil
300g shiitake mushrooms, sliced
2 tablespoons mirin
2.5cm piece of fresh ginger, grated
2 garlic cloves, crushed
1 teaspoon dried chilli flakes
4 tablespoons tamari
1 tablespoon apple cider vinegar
2 tablespoons sesame seeds
Dulse flakes, to taste

Serves 4

Soba noodles are made from buckwheat flour, so they are an interesting alternative to those made from wheat flour. And as an added bonus, they are also gluten free (but check the ingredients on the packaging to ensure they are not made from a mixture of wheat and buckwheat). I always have soba noodles on hand so that when I don't have a lot of time to cook, I can whip up this bowl in a flash and feel good about it. For a heartier meal, add cooked chicken, prawns or tofu.

Cook the noodles according to the packet instructions. Once cooked, put the noodles in a large bowl.

Steam or boil the broccoli for 3 minutes, then add it to the noodle bowl.

Heat a frying pan over a medium to high heat and melt the coconut oil. Fry the mushrooms for about 5–7 minutes until soft, then add to the noodles.

Whisk together the mirin, ginger, garlic, chilli flakes, tamari and apple cider vinegar in a small bowl. Pour it over the noodles and stir to coat the noodles, broccoli and mushrooms with the dressing. Sprinkle with sesame seeds and dulse flakes and serve. Yes, it's that simple!

SOME SAY SHIITAKE MUSHROOMS HAVE BAGS MORE FLAVOUR THAN STANDARD WHITE MUSHROOMS. THEY CONTAIN 65 PERCENT COPPER, WHICH IS ESSENTIAL TO THE HEALTH OF OUR IMMUNE SYSTEM, BLOOD VESSELS AND NERVES.

ADZUKI AND QUINOA TEX-MEX CASSEROLE

1 tablespoon coconut oil,
  plus a little extra for brushing
2 garlic cloves, crushed
1 onion, finely chopped
2 jalapeños, deseeded and
  chopped
240ml vegetable stock
2 x 400g tins adzuki beans,
  drained and rinsed
240ml water
170g quinoa
2 spring onions, sliced
1 teaspoon chilli powder
2 teaspoons ground cumin
½ teaspoon cayenne pepper
2 red peppers, deseeded and
  chopped
2 yellow peppers, deseeded
  and chopped
2 tablespoons nutritional yeast
Large handful of fresh
  coriander, chopped

Serves 6

Growing up in the States, we're accustomed to tex-mex cuisine. Unfortunately, most of the tex-mex recipes are loaded with fat, cheese and cream. Sure, it might taste good at the time, but the aftermath is low energy and heaviness. This tex-mex-inspired casserole recipe takes the fat and heaviness out and puts the goodness and lightness back in.

Heat the coconut oil in a frying pan over a medium to high heat and add the garlic, onion and jalapeños. Cook for about 5 minutes, or until the onion becomes translucent. Stir in the vegetable stock and adzuki beans. Use a fork to lightly mash the beans, but leave some whole to create a chunky texture.

Put the 240ml water in a small saucepan and bring to the boil. Add the quinoa, bring back to the boil, cover and simmer for about 20 minutes until the quinoa is cooked. Drain if needed. Once cooked, stir in the spring onions, chilli powder, cumin and cayenne pepper. Preheat the oven to 180°C/Gas 4.

Brush a casserole with a little coconut oil and spoon the black bean mixture over the base of the dish. Top with the quinoa and then the red and yellow peppers. Cover with foil or a lid and bake in the preheated oven for about 20 minutes. Take the foil or lid off and cook for a further 5 minutes until the peppers are slightly browned. Remove from the oven and, while still hot, sprinkle the nutritional yeast and coriander over the top before serving.

JUST A SMALL HANDFUL OF **ADZUKI BEANS** CONTAINS 100 PERCENT OF THE RDA FOR THE TRACE MINERAL MOLYBDENUM, WHICH AIDS LIVER DETOXIFICATION.

DOUBLE-SPROUT SUPERFOOD BOWLS

2 large beetroots, peeled and
 cut into chunks
1 large sweet potato, peeled
 and cut into chunks
100g Brussels sprouts, halved
1 small head of cauliflower,
 cut into small florets
3–4 tablespoons coconut oil,
 melted
1 teaspoon ground cumin
35g goji berries
480ml water
190g brown rice
1 x 400g tin chickpeas,
 drained and rinsed
4 small handfuls of spinach
Large handful of alfalfa sprouts
50g walnuts, roughly chopped
1 pear, grated
Sea salt and freshly ground
 black pepper

For the dressing
½ avocado, peeled, pitted
 and chopped
Juice of 1 lime
2 tablespoons apple cider
 vinegar
1 garlic clove
1 tablespoon raw honey
¼ teaspoon ground cumin
1 tablespoon tamari
2 tablespoons water

Large baking tray lined with
 aluminium foil

Serves 4

If you're feeling a bit low in energy and perhaps haven't been exactly healthy recently, then this bowl is for you. It contains nutrient-packed fruit, veg and wholegrains to re-nourish your body when you need that super-charge.

Preheat the oven to 200°C/Gas 6. Coat the beetroots, sweet potato, Brussels sprouts and cauliflower in the melted coconut oil and season with the cumin and some salt and black pepper. Put the vegetables on the prepared baking tray and roast in the preheated oven for 30–40 minutes until tender and cooked.

Soak the goji berries in water for 10 minutes, then drain and set aside.

Meanwhile, bring the 480ml water to the boil in a saucepan, then add the brown rice. Reduce the heat to low, cover and simmer for 45–60 minutes until all the water has been absorbed. Once cooked, leave the rice to cool.

Put all the dressing ingredients in a blender or food processor and blitz until smooth.

Evenly distribute the rice, roasted vegetables, chickpeas, spinach, alfalfa sprouts, walnuts, grated pear and soaked goji berries between serving bowls. Drizzle the dressing over the top and tuck in!

BRUSSELS SPROUTS ARE A CRUCIFEROUS VEGETABLE RELATED TO THE CABBAGE. SMALL BUT MIGHTY, A QUARTER OF THEIR CALORIES COMES FROM PROTEIN.

MUNG BEAN, SWEET POTATO AND POMEGRANATE CASSEROLE

1 tablespoon coconut oil
1 teaspoon fenugreek seeds
1 teaspoon cumin seeds
3 garlic cloves, crushed
3cm piece of fresh ginger, grated
2 large green chillies, sliced
2 small onions, diced
2 red peppers, deseeded and chopped
2 sweet potatoes, cut into chunks
1 teaspoon ground turmeric
250g mung beans
1 litre vegetable stock
2 large handfuls of spinach
3 large tomatoes, cut into chunks
Juice of 1 lime
Seeds from 1 pomegranate
Sea salt and freshly ground black pepper

Serves 6

I like cooking with mung beans because they are particularly affordable compared to other beans, and they are a nutritional powerhouse packed with vitamins A, B, C and E as well as minerals such as potassium, magnesium, iron and calcium.

Heat the coconut oil in a large saucepan, then add the fenugreek and cumin seeds and cook for about 2 minutes until you smell the lovely fragrance of the spices.

Add the garlic, ginger, chillies, onions and red peppers and sauté for 5–7 minutes. Toss in the sweet potatoes and turmeric and cook for about 2 minutes.

Stir in the mung beans and vegetable stock. Bring to the boil, then simmer for about 45 minutes, or until the beans are cooked.

Lastly, add the spinach and tomatoes and cook for about 7–10 minutes until both are soft.

Squeeze the lime juice over the casserole and top with the pomegranate seeds. Season with some salt and black pepper and serve.

MUNG BEANS ARE A GOOD SOURCE OF ISOFLAVONES, WHICH ARE A CLASS OF PHYTOESTROGEN THAT HELPS TO REGULATE HORMONAL ACTIVITY.

SWEET RHUBARB, APRICOT AND QUINOA STEW

1 tablespoon cumin seeds
1 tablespoon cardamom pods
2 tablespoons coconut oil
1 large onion, finely chopped
3 garlic cloves, crushed
5cm piece of fresh ginger,
  grated
5 sticks of rhubarb, sliced
1 small butternut squash,
  cut into 2–3cm cubes
  (no need to peel)
15–20 dried apricots
200g quinoa
900ml water
3 tablespoons raw honey
Handful of fresh flat-leaf
  parsley, chopped, to garnish
Sea salt and freshly ground
  black pepper

Serves 6

When rhubarb is in season, well – it's delicious! And rhubarb doesn't have to be put in just puddings and cakes either. It can be used in main meals, too. I particularly like this dish when I'm craving something sweet. Squash is a wonderful sweet vegetable to help curb those sugar cravings, and combine that with the apricots and honey and you've got one healthy sugar fix!

Grind the spices with a pestle and mortar to release the fragrance, then pick out the cardamom shells. Heat the coconut oil in a large saucepan or frying pan. When melted, stir in the ground spices and cook for about 5 minutes. Add the onion, garlic and ginger and stir into the spices for about 2 minutes. Add the rhubarb, butternut squash and apricots and mix well.

Add the quinoa and 900ml water, cover and simmer for about 25 minutes, or until the quinoa is cooked and the squash is soft. Season with some salt and black pepper and stir in the honey. Top with the parsley before serving, and dig in.

ONE SERVING OF COOKED RHUBARB CONTAINS JUST AS MUCH CALCIUM AS ONE SERVING OF MILK.

CASHEW AND CORN SOUP WITH BROCCOLI ALMOND PURÉE

2 tablespoons coconut oil
2 onions, chopped
4 large garlic cloves, chopped
1 teaspoons ground turmeric
1 teaspoon paprika
1 teaspoon ground cumin
170g cashews, soaked in water
  for 4–5 hours
500g sweetcorn
2 litres vegetable stock
Sea salt and freshly ground
  black pepper

For the broccoli almond purée

2 small heads of broccoli,
  cut into florets
60ml almond milk, plus extra
  if needed
2 tablespoons olive oil

Serves 6–8

As odd as might sound to have a nut-based soup, it is delicious, creamy and totally refuelling. Plus, I love that it also includes some all-important greens in the form of the broccoli purée. Making a big batch of it is enough to refuel me at lunchtime and fill up all four kids in the evening.

For the purée, bring a large saucepan of water to the boil and blanch the broccoli for 2–3 minutes. Strain the water from the broccoli and run cool water over the florets. Put the blanched broccoli, almond milk and olive oil in a blender or food processor and blitz until smooth. Add more almond milk as needed. Put to one side.

Heat a large soup pot over a medium heat and melt the coconut oil. Add the onions and garlic and fry for 5 minutes. Add the turmeric, paprika and cumin, stirring well to coat the onion and garlic. Add the soaked cashews, sweetcorn and vegetable stock and bring to the boil, then reduce the heat to low and simmer for 1 hour.

Use a hand-held blender (or a blender or food processor) to blend the soup until it is smooth, then season to taste. Pour into bowls and garnish with the broccoli almond purée.

CHOLESTEROL – FREE CASHEWS ARE PARTICULARLY RICH IN MAGNESIUM, WHICH, JUST LIKE CALCIUM, IS NECESSARY FOR STRONG BONES.

BULGHUR-WHEAT AND NORI SUSHI WITH CREAMY WASABI DIPPING SAUCE

200g bulghur wheat
400ml water
4 nori sheets
2 baby gem lettuces
1 small cucumber, sliced into
   5cm-long matchsticks
4 radishes, thinly sliced
1 carrot, grated
1 large avocado, peeled, pitted
   and thinly sliced
Toasted sesame seeds,
   for sprinkling
Sea salt, to taste

**For the creamy wasabi
   dipping sauce**
½ teaspoon wasabi powder
1½ tablespoons brown rice
   vinegar
1½ tablespoons tamari
1½ tablespoons tahini
½ teaspoon sea salt

Sushi mat

Serves 4–6

Remember, white rice has a lot of its nutritional profile stripped away, so whenever possible, I try to substitute white rice with any wholegrain. If you would prefer to use a gluten-free grain for this recipe, then quinoa is a great alternative, too.

Put the bulghur wheat in a saucepan and add the 400ml water. Bring to the boil, then reduce to a simmer, cover and cook for 15–20 minutes until all the water has been absorbed and the bulghur is tender. Transfer to a bowl and leave to cool.

Place a nori sheet, matt side up, on a sushi mat. Using wet hands, spread a quarter of the bulghur wheat over the nori sheet in a thin, even layer, but make sure to leave a 5cm border at the top.

Arrange a quarter of the vegetables lengthways, starting with the baby gem lettuce, across the centre of the bulghur wheat and sprinkle with sesame seeds. Pick up the edge of the mat closest to you and start to roll it away from you while holding onto the filling. Pull the mat gently while rolling, in order to get a firm roll. Keep rolling until you have a nice neat, tight roll. Use a wet and very sharp knife to neatly cut the nori roll into pieces, then arrange on a platter. Repeat with the remaining nori sheets and vegetables.

Whisk all the sauce ingredients together in a small bowl and serve with the sushi for dipping.

BY EATING 2 SHEETS OF NORI SEAWEED, YOU GET AS MUCH IRON AS YOU WOULD FROM DRINKING 1 GLASS OF MILK OR EATING 1 EGG.

MACADAMIA PESTO ON WHOLEGRAIN PASTA

Homemade pesto is so delicious! My 13-year-old son, Jack, is obsessed with pesto and would be very, very happy if he could have it every night for supper! So, this twist on the same old basil, pine nut and olive oil combination brought a huge smile to his face and I think it will bring one to yours, too.

500g wholegrain pasta

For the pesto
2 large handfuls of fresh basil, leaves only
100g macadamia nuts
1 tablespoon nutritional yeast
1 garlic clove
100ml olive oil
Large handful of fresh flat-leaf parsley, leaves only

Serves 4

Put all the pesto ingredients in a food processor and whizz together until you achieve the consistency of your choice.

Cook the wholewheat pasta according to the packet instructions until al dente. Stir the pesto through and serve immediately.

ALTHOUGH THEY ARE ONE OF THE MOST CALORIFIC NUTS, MACADAMIAS CONTAIN THE HIGHEST AMOUNT OF HEART-HEALTHY MONOUNSATURATED FAT PER SERVING, WHICH HELPS TO LOWER BAD 'LDL' CHOLESTEROL.

KALE, **FIG** AND WALNUT RISOTTO

I created this recipe because I got bored of mushroom risotto. Make it on a 'date night' or double and triple it for a dinner party. **(See photograph on page 97.)**

1 tablespoon coconut oil
1 onion, chopped
1 garlic clove, crushed
170g buckwheat groats
500ml vegetable stock, plus extra if needed
100g walnuts
2 tablespoons nutritional yeast
2 large handfuls of kale, stems removed and roughly chopped
5 figs, quartered

Serves 2

Melt the coconut oil a large saucepan over a medium heat and fry the onion and garlic for 5 minutes, or until the onion is translucent. Add the buckwheat and sauté for a couple of minutes until well coated, stirring. Add the stock and bring to the boil, then reduce the heat and simmer for 25–30 minutes. Add more stock if looking dry.

Dry roast the walnuts in a small pan for a few minutes over a medium heat.

Add the yeast, kale and toasted walnuts to the cooked buckwheat mixture and stir. Garnish with the figs and serve.

HIGH-FIBRE **FIGS** ACT AS A NATURAL LAXATIVE AND HELP TO NOURISH THE INTESTINES.

THAI COCONUT NOODLE BOWL WITH PAK CHOI AND MUSHROOMS

2 x 400ml tins coconut milk
240ml vegetable stock
1 tablespoon dried coriander
6 lemongrass stalks
1 large onion, thinly sliced
2–3 garlic cloves, crushed
1 tablespoon shredded kaffir lime leaves, plus extra to garnish (optional)
50g coconut palm sugar
Large handful of portabellini mushrooms, sliced
3 tablespoons tamari
Juice of 2 limes
Juice of 1 lemon
100g pak choi, roughly chopped
50g thin rice or soba noodles
1 red chilli, sliced, to garnish
Fresh coriander, to garnish

Serves 4

Asian food is cooked with fantastically aromatic flavours. Although there is traditionally a heavy emphasis on fish and meat, you can create an amazing Thai dish, like this one, without using any. However, feel free to add in some prawns or cooked chicken if you feel the need.

Pour the coconut milk and stock into a large saucepan and stir in the dried coriander, lemongrass, onion, garlic, kaffir lime leaves and coconut palm sugar. Bring the contents of the pan to a simmer and cook for 15–20 minutes. Strain through a sieve into a clean saucepan and discard the ingredients left in the sieve.

Add the sliced mushrooms, tamari, lime and lemon juice, pak choi and rice noodles and bring to a simmer again. After 3–4 minutes, your soup is ready.

Serve in soup bowls and garnish with fresh coriander leaves, red chilli and maybe some more chopped kaffir lime leaves.

PAK CHOI IS A TYPE OF CHINESE CABBAGE THAT IS EXTREMELY LOW IN CALORIES, HAS HARDLY A TRACE OF FAT, YET DELIVERS ALMOST ALL THE ESSENTIAL VITAMINS AND MINERALS.

SPICY TOFU CURRY WITH COCONUT AND CARDAMOM

3 tablespoons coconut oil
2 onions, finely chopped
3cm piece of fresh ginger, grated
1 teaspoon ground cumin
¼ teaspoon ground cardamom
2 teaspoons ground coriander
2 teaspoons ground turmeric
2 teaspoons chilli powder
450g firm tofu, cut into small chunks
100g (block) coconut cream
475ml boiling water
Lime juice, to taste
Sea salt and freshly ground black pepper
Brown rice or soba noodles, to serve

Serves 4

Although this recipe was originally intended to have prawns in it, I've used tofu instead, but you can, of course, add whichever you would prefer – they're both extremely satisfying.

Melt the coconut oil in a large frying pan over a medium heat. Add the onion and ginger and fry for 2–3 minutes. While continuing to fry, add the cumin, cardamom, coriander, turmeric and chilli powder. Stir the contents of the pan well, then add the tofu. Reduce the heat to low and leave to cook gently while you create the coconut milk.

Mix the block of coconut cream with the 475ml boiling water in a jug. Stir well, then pour this into the frying pan. Turn the heat back up to a medium and allow everything to cook together for 5–10 minutes. Squeeze over the lime juice and season to taste.

Serve over brown rice or soba noodles – both are equally delicious!

This is the kind of meal you need when you're poorly and your body craves strong flavours accompanied by sustaining rice or noodles.

CARDAMOM IS FANTASTIC FOR INDIGESTION AND HEARTBURN RELIEF. YOU CAN EVEN CHEW A FEW SEEDS TO HELP AS WELL!

RED VELVET LENTILS ON BROWN RICE

2 tablespoons coconut oil
1½ teaspoons black mustard
  seeds
1½ teaspoons cumin seeds
1 onion, chopped
2.5cm piece of fresh ginger,
  grated
2 teaspoons ground turmeric
2 teaspoons ground cumin
1 x 400g tin chopped tomatoes
400g red lentils
2 litres vegetable stock
1 cinnamon stick
480ml water
190g brown rice
Juice of 1 lime
1 tablespoon raw honey
Small handful of fresh
  coriander, chopped,
  to garnish

Serves 4

My 10-year-old son, William, calls this dish his 'favourite meal in the whole wide world' and he can actually polish it off in no time, and then go on to seconds and even thirds if there's any left!

Melt the coconut oil in a large saucepan over a medium heat and add the mustard and cumin seeds. Fry until the seeds begin to pop, then quickly add the onion, ginger, turmeric and cumin. Continue to sauté for a further 2–3 minutes, then add the chopped tomatoes. Cook for 2 minutes, then add the lentils, vegetable stock and cinnamon stick. Bring to the boil, then lower the heat, cover and simmer for a good 30 minutes.

Meanwhile, bring the water to the boil in another saucepan and add the brown rice. Reduce the heat, cover and simmer for 45–60 minutes, until the rice is tender.

After 30 minutes, the lentils should be tender. Remove the cinnamon stick and stir in the lime juice and honey.

Spoon the rice into serving bowls and top with the lentil mixture. Garnish with the coriander and serve.

OUT OF ALL LEGUMES AND NUTS, LENTILS CONTAIN THE THIRD HIGHEST AMOUNT OF PROTEIN.

MUSHROOM, BROCCOLI AND COCONUT CURRY

2 tablespoons coconut oil
1 teaspoon cumin seeds
1 onion, chopped
2 garlic cloves, finely chopped
3cm piece of fresh ginger, grated
2 red chillies, finely chopped
1 teaspoon ground turmeric
1 teaspoon ground cumin
1 teaspoon curry powder
250g button mushrooms, sliced
1 head of broccoli, cut into florets
4 large tomatoes, finely chopped
1 x 400ml tin coconut milk
400ml water
4 large handfuls of spinach
2 large handfuls of kale, roughly torn and stems removed
Handful of fresh coriander, chopped, to garnish
50g toasted almonds, roughly chopped, to garnish
Sea salt and freshly ground black pepper
Brown rice or soba noodles, to serve

Serves 4

Everyone loves a curry and this is a twist on the classic veggie variety. I've included the dark green leafy veg – broccoli, spinach AND kale – that we ideally want to have every day, as well as some mushrooms and tomatoes, which provide a different texture and colour to the dish.

Melt the coconut oil in a large saucepan over a medium heat and add the cumin seeds. Fry until the seeds begin to pop and become fragrant, then quickly add the onion, garlic, ginger and red chillies and fry for 1–2 minutes.

Add all the ground spices and cook for 5–7 minutes, or until the onion is translucent. Add the mushrooms, broccoli, tomatoes, coconut milk and 400ml water and cook for a further 10–15 minutes until the mushrooms are soft.

Gently stir in the spinach and kale and allow to wilt.

Serve over brown rice or soba noodles and garnish with the chopped coriander and toasted almonds.

BROCCOLI STANDS OUT FROM ALL THE CRUCIFEROUS VEGETABLES AS HAVING THE HIGHEST CONCENTRATION OF VITAMIN C.

BUTTERNUT SQUASH AND
CHILLI SOUP WITH SPELT

2 tablespoons coconut oil
2 onions, chopped
2–3 garlic cloves, crushed
1 teaspoon ground turmeric
½ teaspoon dried chilli flakes
1 teaspoon ground cinnamon
1kg butternut squash, peeled
   and cut into chunks (reserving
   the seeds)
1 litre vegetable stock
175g pearled spelt
Handful of fresh coriander,
   chopped, to garnish

Serves 3–4

Here's a great recipe if you're looking for a meal to cheer you up on a cold day. Not only will the warming soup feel good in your body, your body will welcome the fantastic nutrition in this soup, too!

Melt the coconut oil in a large saucepan over a medium heat and add the chopped onions. Fry for 2–3 minutes, then add the garlic, turmeric, chilli flakes and cinnamon. Stir to coat the onion and garlic with the spices for a few minutes.

Add the butternut squash, stir again, then add the vegetable stock and spelt. Bring to the boil, then reduce the heat and simmer for 30 minutes.

Meanwhile, preheat the oven to 180°C/Gas 4. Put the reserved butternut squash seeds on a baking tray and toast in the preheated oven for 10 minutes. Once toasted, put to one side.

When the spelt and squash are cooked through, use a hand-held blender (or a blender or food processor) to whizz until the soup is puréed but still a bit chunky. Garnish with fresh coriander and the toasted squash seeds to serve.

CHILLI FLAKES CAN HELP BOOST YOUR METABOLISM AND DECREASE HUNGER.

SIDES

I love side dishes, and I never go to a
restaurant without ordering at least
two. And I make sure to always have a
nutritional powerhouse of a side at home.
It can be as simple as steamed spinach,
but I always try to get it in. It's especially
important, if you are having meat as
your main dish, to accompany it with a
nutritious side in order to fight the free
radicals that form in the body when eating
meat. Stocking up on some of the dishes
in this chapter will help to eradicate those
free radicals, once and for all.

THREE TYPES OF HUMMOUS

AVOCADO HUMMOUS

1 x 400g tin chickpeas, drained
2 ripe avocados, peeled, pitted
   and chopped
Juice of 1 lime
Juice of 1 lemon
Large handful of fresh coriander
4 garlic cloves, crushed
2 tablespoons olive oil
2 tablespoons tahini
1 teaspoon sea salt

GREEN PEA HUMMOUS

500g peas (or frozen are fine)
Juice of 2 lemons
3 garlic cloves, crushed
1 tablespoon olive oil
Small handful of fresh coriander
2 tablespoons tahini
1 teaspoon ground cumin
½ teaspoon cayenne pepper
1 teaspoon sea salt

SMOKED PAPRIKA HUMMOUS

1 x 400g tin chickpeas, drained
3 garlic cloves, crushed
Juice of ½ lemon
2 teaspoons smoked paprika
2 tablespoons olive oil
2 tablespoons tahini
Small handful of fresh flat-leaf
   parsley
1 tablespoon apple cider
   vinegar
1 teaspoon sea salt

All serve 4

I love hummous, but it doesn't always have to be made the same ol' way! Yes, chickpeas are wonderful, but if you want to spice it up a bit and do something different, then whip up these three variations for something that's yummy and, of course, healthy. Dunk any raw veggies into your hummous or spread it over a piece of wholegrain bread – I love rye! And, if you want to make it even more interesting, top with red pepper strips or black olives. You can also try spreading your hummous over a piece of grilled chicken to jazz it up.

If using chickpeas in any of these recipes, rinse them well in water first.

To make any of the three variations, throw all the ingredients into a food processor and whizz until smooth. Serve with fresh, colourful crudités.

TAHINI IS ONE OF THE BEST SOURCES OF CALCIUM OUT THERE, AND IS A HIGHER SOURCE OF PROTEIN THAN MOST NUTS!

BLACK RICE, KALE, SEED AND RED GRAPE PILAF

1 litre vegetable stock
380g black rice
1 tablespoon coconut oil
1 onion, chopped
2 garlic cloves, finely chopped
1 teaspoon ground cumin
1½ teaspoons paprika
½ teaspoon ground turmeric
120ml apple cider vinegar
2 large handfuls of kale,
   roughly chopped and stems
   removed
200g red seedless grapes,
   halved
55g sunflower seeds
Sea salt and freshly ground
   black pepper

Serves 4–6

You can make this recipe with any wholegrain that you have to hand in your pantry, such as brown rice, quinoa, bulghur wheat, etc. However, I love the stunning colour of the black rice with the dark green kale and red grapes. It's a very pretty side dish! It marries well with a simple piece of steamed fish, or try it with my Cashew and Corn Soup with Broccoli Almond Purée (see page 115).

Bring the vegetable stock to the boil, then add the black rice. Reduce the heat to low, then cover and simmer for 45–60 minutes until tender.

Meanwhile, melt the coconut oil in a large frying pan over a medium heat and add the onion and garlic. Fry for 5–7 minutes, or until the onion is translucent.

Add the cumin, paprika, turmeric and apple cider vinegar to the onions and garlic, combine and stir for 1–2 minutes. Add the kale and stir through. Once the kale is soft and the liquid has been absorbed, remove the pan from the heat.

Mix the mushroom and kale mixture with the cooked rice, grapes and sunflower seeds in a large bowl. Season with salt and pepper, toss well and serve.

RED GRAPES ARE FULL OF VITAMIN K, WHICH IS A FAT-SOLUBLE VITAMIN STORED IN OUR BODY'S FAT TISSUE AND LIVER. IT PLAYS A KEY ROLE IN BLOOD CLOTTING.

WARM MILLET, BEETROOT AND BROCCOLI SALAD

2 medium beetroots, peeled
  and cut into chunks
1 head of broccoli, cut into
  florets
1 tablespoon coconut oil,
  melted
2 tablespoons tamari
1 teaspoon ground cumin
200g tinned black beans,
  drained and rinsed
480ml vegetable stock
200g millet
35g pumpkin or sunflower
  seeds
Sea salt and freshly ground
  black pepper

For the dressing
2 tablespoons tamari
1 tablespoon tahini
1 tablespoon raw honey
2 tablespoons apple cider
  vinegar
Squeeze of lemon juice
1 teaspoon ground cumin

Serves 4

Millet is another gluten-free grain that is often overlooked. It's been around for centuries, but not until recently has it started to gain popularity as a nutritious but also gluten-free alternative to wheat. This tasty salad goes perfectly with my Mushroom, Broccoli and Coconut Curry (see page 124), or with salmon. **(See photograph on page 129.)**

Preheat the oven to 180°C/Gas 4. Put the beetroots and broccoli on a baking tray and coat with the melted coconut oil, tamari and cumin. Add some salt and black pepper to taste, then roast in the preheated oven for 20 minutes.

Remove the tray from the oven, add the black beans and return to the oven for another 10 minutes.

Meanwhile, bring the vegetable stock to the boil, then add the millet. Bring back to the boil, reduce the heat to low and cover and simmer for 25–30 minutes until the water has been absorbed and the millet is tender.

Transfer the cooked millet to a large bowl and mix in the roasted broccoli, beetroot and black beans.

Combine all the dressing ingredients in a bowl and whisk together. Coat the salad with the dressing and top with pumpkin or sunflower seeds.

NOT ONLY IS MILLET ALKALINE AND EASILY DIGESTIBLE, BUT IT CONTAINS SERATONIN, WHICH HELPS YOUR MOOD.

GINGER AND UMEBOSHI
AUBERGINES WITH MANGO

500g aubergines
About 5 tablespoons coconut oil
2 small onions, chopped
2 garlic cloves, finely chopped
1 red chilli, finely chopped
2cm piece of fresh ginger,
   peeled and grated
¾ teaspoon ground cinnamon
Pinch of ground nutmeg
2 tablespoons umeboshi paste
2 teaspoons coconut palm
   sugar
75ml water
2 small mangoes, peeled,
   pitted and chopped
Sea salt

Serves 4

The idea for this interesting combination came to me as I was staring blankly at the inside of my fridge with not a whole lot of choice! It's an incredibly delicious accompaniment to my Broccoli and Mushroom Soba Noodle Bowl (see page 104), or in fact any lamb dish. **(See photograph on page 129.)**

Cut the aubergines into 1.5cm-thick slices and place them in a glass dish. Sprinkle with sea salt and leave them to sit and sweat for 30 minutes. Towards the end of this time, melt 2 tablespoons of the coconut oil in a large frying pan over a medium heat. Add the onions, garlic, chilli and ginger and fry for 5–7 minutes. Add the cinnamon and nutmeg and fry for an additional 2 minutes.

Using a clean tea towel or some kitchen roll, wipe the salted aubergines until they are dry. Melt 3 tablespoons of the coconut oil in another frying pan over a medium heat, then fry the aubergines for about 10 minutes until they are golden on both sides. Add more coconut oil if needed. Turn the oven on to its lowest setting, put the aubergines in a baking dish and place in the oven to keep warm.

Reheat the onion mixture over a medium heat, then add the umeboshi paste, coconut palm sugar and 75ml water. Stir well and leave the mixture to simmer for 5 minutes. Transfer the mixture to a blender or food processor, add the mango and whizz until smooth. Arrange the aubergines on a platter and drizzle the umeboshi and mango sauce over the top.

AUBERGINES ARE RICH IN AN ANTIOXIDANT CALLED CHLOROGENIC ACID, ADEPT AT FIGHTING FREE RADICALS.

COCONUT, CORN AND HAZELNUT SALAD

3 tablespoons coconut oil
4 ears of corn, shucked
1 small red onion, thinly sliced
40g coconut flakes
75g hazelnuts, toasted
75g sultanas
Small handful of fresh flat-leaf
  parsley, chopped
Juice of 2 limes
Sea salt and freshly ground
  black pepper

Serves 4

I grew up in Illinois, so I was surrounded by corn fields throughout my childhood. In this salad, I use corn fresh from the cob, as nothing tastes better. However, if you are in a real rush, it's fine to use tinned corn. This Illinois-style side dish is very tasty with burgers during those barbecue months. Or try it with my Sweet Rhubarb, Apricot and Quinoa Stew (see page 112).

Melt the coconut oil in a large frying pan over a medium heat. Add the corn, red onion and coconut flakes and stir to coat well with the oil. Cook for 5 minutes, then transfer to a serving bowl.

Add the toasted hazelnuts, sultanas, parsley and lime juice. Stir well and season with salt and black pepper.

CORN IS PACKED WITH LUTEIN AND ZEAXANTHIN WHICH ARE TWO PHYTOCHEMICALS THAT HELP PROMOTE HEALTHY VISION.

CABBAGE, CARROT AND FLAXSEED COLESLAW

1 small savoy cabbage
1 small purple cabbage
Large handful of mangetout
2 carrots, grated
2 small red onions, thinly sliced
2 tablespoons flaxseeds

For the dressing
4 tablespoons olive oil
2 garlic cloves, crushed
Large handful of fresh dill
1 tablespoon Dijon mustard
2 tablespoons apple cider
   vinegar
Juice of 1 lemon

Serves 4–6

There are so many ways to make coleslaw, and often the shop-bought ones are extremely fatty. Making it yourself is a great way to ensure that it stays healthy. Although coleslaw is traditionally served with meat dishes, it's also great to have with pizza or pasta. Pair this lovely, light slaw with some chicken or lamb kebabs, or with my Kale, Fig and Walnut Risotto (see page 119).

Thinly slice both of the cabbages and the mangetout. Put in a large bowl with the grated carrot and red onions and mix well.

Combine all the dressing ingredients in a blender or food processor until smooth. Pour over the coleslaw and mix well. Sprinkle with the flaxseeds.

CABBAGE CONTAINS AN ABUNDANCE OF VITAMIN C. IN FACT, IT'S RICHER IN THIS VITAMIN THAN ORANGES ARE. VITAMIN C IS ONE OF THE BEST ANTIOXIDANTS TO REDUCE FREE RADICALS IN THE BODY.

QUINOA AND SAUTÉED RED CABBAGE WITH ORANGES

1 litre vegetable stock
400g mixed red and white
  quinoa
2 bay leaves
2 tablespoons coconut oil
½ tablespoon black mustard
  seeds
1 tablespoon fennel seeds
2 onions, chopped
4 garlic cloves, finely chopped
½ red cabbage, thinly sliced
2 tablespoons apple cider
  vinegar
4 oranges
Small handful of fresh flat-leaf
  parsley, chopped
Sea salt and freshly ground
  black pepper

Serves 4–6

You can't log on to a healthfood website without reading about the benefits of quinoa – it's everywhere! However, you might not be so familiar with the benefits of red cabbage. This variety of cabbage actually contains a great deal more phytonutrients than green cabbage... so eat up! This dish is perfect as a Sunday lunch accompaniment to roast chicken, or try it with my Mung Bean, Sweet Potato and Pomegranate Casserole (see page 110) for a plant-based Sunday lunch.

Bring the vegetable stock to the boil in a large saucepan and add the quinoa and bay leaves. Reduce the heat to low and simmer for 20–25 minutes until the water has been absorbed and the quinoa is tender.

Melt the coconut oil in a frying pan and fry the black mustard seeds with the fennel seeds. After 3 minutes, add the onions and garlic and fry for 5–7 minutes until the onion has softened. Add the cabbage and apple cider vinegar and continue to fry for another 5 minutes.

Meanwhile, juice 3 of the oranges and segment the last one. Strain the juice into the pan with the red cabbage. Stir well and season with salt and pepper.

Put the quinoa in a large bowl and top with the cabbage, orange segments and chopped parsley.

RED CABBAGE HAS A HIGH CONTENT OF ANTHOCYANINS, A TYPE OF FLAVONOID THAT HAS BEEN LINKED TO CANCER PREVENTION.

ULTIMATE SUPERFOOD SALAD WITH HEMP AND BLUEBERRIES

4 large handfuls of baby
  spinach
1 head of broccoli, cut into
  small florets
1 cooked beetroot, thinly sliced
1 carrot, grated
1 avocado, peeled, pitted and
  sliced
Small handful of fresh mint,
  roughly chopped
Large handful of blueberries
1 tablespoon flaxseeds
1 tablespoon chia seeds
1 tablespoon hemp seeds
Optional: for more Omega
  madness, add a small handful
  of pumpkin and sunflower
  seeds too!

For the blueberry dressing
Large handful of blueberries
Juice of 1 lime
2 tablespoons apple cider
  vinegar
1 tablespoon raw honey
1 tablespoon olive oil
Sea salt and freshly ground
  black pepper

Serves 4

Here we have a super-serious salad with a super-serious dressing. I always want to start my week out on the right foot, and this salad eaten on Monday always helps me to stay focused with what I'm putting in my body during the rest of the week. It is especially good with a steak or simple grilled piece of meat, or pair it with my Macadamia Pesto on Wholegrain Pasta (see page 119).

Lightly toss the spinach, broccoli, beetroot, carrot, avocado, mint and blueberries together in a bowl.

Combine all the dressing ingredients in a blender or food processor and whizz until smooth. Drizzle the dressing over the salad, then sprinkle over all the seeds. Season with salt and black pepper and serve.

HEMP SEEDS BREATHE LIFE INTO ANY DISH. THEY ARE AN EXPLOSION OF OMEGA-6 AND OMEGA-3 FATTY ACIDS TO AID IN HEALTHY HEART AND BRAIN FUNCTION.

TENDERSTEM BROCCOLI, SUN—DRIED TOMATO, GARLIC AND WALNUT SALAD

3 tablespoons coconut oil
6 garlic cloves, thinly sliced
2 large bunches of Tenderstem broccoli
110g sun-dried tomatoes, drained (or if not from a jar, soak in water for 10 minutes and drain)
2 teaspoons dried chilli flakes
100g walnuts, roughly chopped
Sea salt and freshly ground black pepper

Serves 4–6

If you haven't picked up on it yet, I'm obsessed with dark green, leafy vegetables, and finding something different to do with them is super-fun. This recipe came to me as I was staring at my broccoli one day, trying to think of a new way to prepare it. It also makes a great portable lunch. Get this green side in with a steak or, for the all-veggie option, try it with my Butternut Squash and Chilli Soup with Spelt (see page 126).

Melt the coconut oil in a large frying pan over a medium heat, add the garlic and fry for 30 seconds. Be careful that the garlic doesn't begin to go brown.

Add the broccoli and sauté for 2 minutes before adding the sun-dried tomatoes. Sprinkle the chilli flakes over the broccoli and lower the heat slightly. Continue to sauté for an additional 3 minutes, then transfer to a bowl.

In a separate dry pan, toast the walnuts for just 1–2 minutes so that they brown ever so slightly. Combine with the broccoli, season with salt and pepper and serve immediately.

IN THE WINTER, GARLIC IS A GREAT FOOD FOR BOOSTING YOUR IMMUNE SYSTEM TO FIGHT OFF COLDS AND FLU.

MIXED **BEAN**, AVOCADO AND CLEMENTINE SALAD WITH TAHINI DRESSING

For the bean salad
1 x 400g tin mixed beans,
  drained and rinsed
100g green beans, cooked
2 handfuls of flaked almonds,
  lightly toasted
1 head of romaine lettuce,
  chopped
1 large avocado, peeled, pitted
  and sliced
2 clementines, peeled and
  segmented
1 yellow pepper, chopped
Large handful of fresh
  coriander, chopped

For the tahini dressing
2 tablespoons tahini
2 tablespoons apple cider
  vinegar
2 tablespoons tamari
2 tablespoons lemon juice
1 tablespoon raw honey

Serves 4

Tahini is one of my favourite ingredients to use when I'm making a dressing. It provides a creamy texture and sweet, nutty flavour and is great over any roasted vegetables or salad. This protein-packed side dish goes perfectly with an oily fish like tuna, salmon or mackerel, or with my Red Peppers Stuffed with Bulghur Wheat and Pistachios (see page 101). **(See photograph on page 143.)**

For the salad, simply combine all the ingredients in a large bowl.

The dressing is just as easy! Combine all the dressing ingredients in a small mixing bowl and whisk together by hand. Pour the dressing over the bean salad and toss well, then serve.

GREEN BEANS CONTAIN EXCELLENT LEVELS OF VITAMIN A, WHICH IS KNOWN TO HELP COMBAT WRINKLES, FINE LINES AND AGE SPOTS.

POMEGRANATE, CUCUMBER AND TOMATO SALAD

1 large pomegranate
1 small cucumber, chopped
4 large tomatoes, cut into
  chunks
1 hot red chilli, deseeded and
  thinly sliced
1 red pepper, chopped
Large handful of fresh mint,
  roughly chopped
Large handful of fresh
  coriander, roughly chopped
Juice of 1 lime
Drizzle of olive oil

Serves 4

This is a brilliantly easy recipe that you can whip up in no time. It's completely raw, which means that all the crucial enzymes that we need are kept intact and greatly appreciated by our bodies. Top some steamed fish with this salad for some texture and yumminess, or use it as a salsa and pair it with my Adzuki and Quinoa Tex-Mex Casserole (see page 107).

Cut the pomegranate in half and get your fingers in there to prise all of the seeds free. Ensure that you pull away and discard all the pith as you go.

Mix the cucumber, tomato, chilli, red pepper, mint and coriander together in a bowl. Add the pomegranate seeds, then add the juice of the lime and a drizzle of olive oil and toss everything together. Yes, it's that simple and it's super-yummy.

This so straightforward; the only thing likely to take time is getting the seeds out of the pomegranate! When you've cut it in half, hit the fruit with a utensil to dislodge the seeds.

CUCUMBERS ARE 95 PERCENT WATER, WHICH HELPS TO KEEP OUR BODIES HYDRATED WHILE AT THE SAME TIME ELIMINATING TOXINS.

BEETROOT, CELERIAC AND FIG SALAD

3 large beetroots, peeled and
cut into chunks
½ celeriac, trimmed and cut
into chunks
Large handful of fresh flat-leaf
parsley, roughly chopped
Large handful of fresh
coriander, roughly chopped
5 figs, quartered
Sea salt and freshly ground
black pepper

For the lime dressing
Juice and zest of 1 lime
3cm piece of fresh ginger,
peeled and minced
¼ teaspoon ground cumin
¼ teaspoon ground cinnamon
2 tablespoons olive oil
2 tablespoons apple cider
vinegar

Serves 4

When I'm craving something that's healthy and light to satisfy my taste buds, sometimes I find that a mundane salad doesn't cut it. Keeping things interesting in the kitchen is the key to sticking to a healthy diet and this is the kind of salad that will help you do just that. This is another good side to serve with steamed fish – sea bass or bream are perfect. Or, to keep it plant-based and colourful, serve it with my Thai Coconut Noodle Bowl with Pak Choi and Mushrooms (see page 120). It is an absolutely stunning salad in both appearance and flavour!

Fill a large saucepan with about 2cm water and heat over a medium heat. Add the beetroot and cook for about 20 minutes. Drain and put in a large bowl.

Add another 2cm water to the empty pan and heat over a medium heat. Add the celeriac and cook for about 15 minutes. Drain and leave to cool in a separate bowl.

Once the beetroot and celeriac have cooled, add the parsley, coriander and figs to the large bowl, along with the celeriac.

Whisk together all the dressing ingredients in a small bowl. Drizzle over the beetroot and celeriac salad and season with salt and pepper before serving.

BEETROOT IS FANTASTIC FOR INCREASING YOUR STAMINA AND HELPING YOUR MUSCLES WORK HARDER FOR LONGER.

ASPARAGUS, BROCCOLI AND CORIANDER SALAD WITH WALNUTS

2 tablespoons coconut oil
12 spears of asparagus, sliced into 2cm lengths
½ head of broccoli, cut into small florets
55g walnuts, chopped
90g black olives
Handful of fresh coriander, chopped
Grated zest and juice of 1 lemon
1 shallot, finely chopped
Sea salt

Serves 4

I like to chop up my asparagus to make a more manageable salad, but you can keep the asparagus spears whole if you're after something more elegant. Serve this with sausages or my Red Velvet Lentils on Brown Rice (see page 123).

Melt the coconut oil in a large frying pan over a medium to high heat. Add the asparagus and broccoli florets with a pinch of sea salt. Coat the asparagus and broccoli with the coconut oil, cover the pan with a lid and cook for 2 minutes. Remove the vegetables from the pan and place them in a large bowl. Add the walnuts, olives and coriander to the bowl.

Combine the lemon juice and zest with the shallots in a small bowl and whisk well. Pour the dressing over the salad and serve.

ASPARAGUS IS A WONDERFUL SOURCE OF VITAMIN B6, CALCIUM, ZINC AND MAGNESIUM.

PAPRIKA PARSNIP AND SWEET POTATO CHIPS

3 large sweet potatoes, cut into 7cm batons
3 large parsnips, cut into 7cm batons
1 large garlic clove, crushed
3 tablespoons coconut oil, melted
2 teaspoons paprika
Sea salt and freshly ground black pepper

Serves 4–6

A healthier version of the typical chips. Not only are parsnips and sweet potatoes packed with goodness, but baking chips in coconut oil rather than frying them in refined oil is much better for your heart and your health! These chips are sooooo good with beefburgers or with my Beetroot, Quinoa, Black Bean and Flaxseed Burgers (see page 103).

Preheat the oven to 200°C/Gas 6.

Combine all the ingredients in a bowl and mix together so that the parsnips and sweet potatoes are completely coated.

Spread the chips out in a single layer on a baking tray. Roast in the preheated oven for 10 minutes until the chips are lightly browned. Flip them over and roast for an additional 10–15 minutes on the other side. Season with salt and pepper and serve.

A RELATIVE OF CARROTS AND PARSLEY, PARSNIPS ARE PACKED WITH POTASSIUM AND FOLATES, BOTH OF WHICH ARE IMPORTANT NUTRIENTS FOR CARDIOVASCULAR HEALTH.

SPICED COCONUT KALE WITH AVOCADO

Bunch of kale, torn into pieces and chunky stems removed
40g coconut flakes
1 avocado, peeled, pitted and diced
Large handful of flaked almonds, toasted

For the dressing
1 shallot, finely chopped
Juice of 1 lemon
2 tablespoons olive oil
1 tablespoon apple cider vinegar
1 teaspoon dried chilli flakes
1 teaspoon maple syrup

Serves 4

The key to making a proper kale salad taste good is not to cook the kale! You just need to give it some love and soften it with an acidic ingredient or dressing. In my view, this side is perfect for any meat or fish dish. Or try it with my Spicy Tofu Curry with Coconut and Cardamom (see page 122).

Whisk the dressing ingredients together in a small bowl. Once combined, put the kale in a large serving bowl and pour half the dressing over the top. Use your hands to massage the dressing into the kale for a few minutes in order to soften it.

Add the coconut flakes, avocado and flaked almonds and mix together well. Pour in the rest of the dressing and serve.

MANY PEOPLE AVOID EATING AVOCADO, AS THEY THINK IT WILL MAKE THEM PUT ON WEIGHT. HOWEVER, RESEARCH HAS SHOWN THAT THE MONOUNSATURATED FATTY ACIDS FOUND IN AVOCADO ARE MORE LIKELY TO BE USED AS SLOW-BURNING ENERGY THAN STORED AS BODY FAT.

CANTALOUPE MELON AND BLUEBERRY SALAD WITH AVOCADO LIME DRESSING

1 cantaloupe melon, cubed
200g blueberries
Large handful of fresh mint, chopped
Pinch of ground cinnamon

For the avocado lime dressing
½ avocado, peeled, pitted and chopped
1 tablespoon raw honey
Juice of 1 lime
Small handful of fresh mint
2 tablespoons water

Serves 4

Here is a great summer salad to eat when the sun is shining. Looking at this salad will no doubt bring a smile to your face, as not only is it delicious, but something about a fruit salad that's light and refreshing always makes me feel good! This is a light side that goes amazingly well with steamed fish or my Double-Sprout Superfood Bowls (see page 109).

Combine the cantaloupe, blueberries, mint and cinnamon in a large serving bowl.

Put all the dressing ingredients in a food processor and blend until smooth. Thoroughly coat the salad with the dressing and serve.

100G CANTALOUPE MELON CONTAINS 110 PERCENT OF THE RDA FOR VITAMIN A WHICH, AS WE KNOW, IS A POWERFUL ANTIOXIDANT FOR MAINTAINING HEALTHY VISION, MUCUS MEMBRANES AND SKIN.

SWEET TREATS

Of course, this is my favourite chapter and that's perhaps why sweet treats, puddings, desserts – whatever you want to call them – are always in the back of the book; because we save the best for last. All my recipes are made with natural sweeteners, wholegrains, fruits and even some vegetables, too. Sweet treats do not have to be made with refined sugar, butter and white flour to taste good. Those ingredients zap your energy and, personally, I want a treat that's going to give me energy, not take it away. I think you'll see what I mean after you try a few of these recipes.

SUPER NUT-BUTTER CUPS WITH MACA AND LUCUMA

For the chocolate sauce
200g cacao butter
150–180g cacao powder
4 tablespoons raw honey
1½ tablespoons lucuma powder
1½ tablespoons carob powder
1 teaspoon maca powder
¼ teaspoon sea salt

For the almond butter filling
120g almond butter
1 tablespoon raw honey
1 tablespoon lucuma powder

Cupcake tray(s) lined with
  12–16 paper cupcake cases

Makes 12–16

Growing up in America, my hands-down top treat was Reese's peanut butter cups; they are so good. However, they are also unhealthy in every way. So, I set out to invent my own super-healthy version that, in my mind, tastes just as good, if not better, than what I ate as a kid.

Melt the cacao butter in a saucepan over a low to medium heat. Add the rest of the chocolate sauce ingredients and mix until combined.

Spoon in enough chocolate sauce to cover the bottom of each cupcake case set in the cupcake tray. You will only need to use about one-third of the sauce for this. Set the remaining sauce aside. Transfer the tray to the fridge for about 15 minutes, or until the sauce has solidified.

For the almond filling, combine all the ingredients in a small bowl until it looks like a dough. Take good heaped teaspoons of dough and roll them into balls. Then, use your hands to flatten the balls into discs to just less than the diameter of the base of the cupcake cases. Add these almond-butter discs to the cases and spoon the remainder of the chocolate sauce over the top, covering the almond butter fillings completely.

Return the tray to the fridge for 1 hour to set. Once set, you can remove the cases from the tray and store in an airtight container in the fridge for 3 to 4 days.

A ROOT GROWN IN THE MOUNTAINS OF PERU, MACA IS KNOWN FOR INCREASING STAMINA AND ENERGY LEVELS.

MATCHA COCONUT ICE CREAM

This is a lovely, rich and creamy ice cream without the dairy or refined sugar. Green tea (i.e. matcha) ice cream is actually a rather popular pudding at Asian restaurants, but now you can easily make it at home and know that it's packed with goodness.

1 x 400ml tin coconut milk
2 frozen bananas
2 tablespoons matcha (green tea) powder
4 dates, pitted
4 tablespoons maple syrup
6 ice cubes
½ teaspoon xanthan gum

Serves 2–3

Combine all the ingredients in a blender or food processor, then pour into a freezerproof container with a lid. Cover, then freeze for a few hours until solid.

MINT COCOCHIP ICE CREAM

I absolutely love mint – on my potatoes, in tea, in my smoothies and soups, and now in my ice cream! I dare you to make this for dinner when you've got friends coming round – and then tell them how it's made without dairy or refined sugar. They will love you forever and beg for the recipe!

2 frozen bananas
1 x 400ml tin coconut milk
½ teaspoon vanilla extract
2 avocados, peeled, pitted and chopped
8 drops of peppermint essential oil
Small handful of spinach
Large handful of cacao nibs
8 large fresh mint leaves
4 dates, pitted
6 ice cubes

Serves 4

Combine all the ingredients in a blender or food processor, then pour into a freezerproof container with a lid. Fold in the cacao nibs. Freeze for a couple of hours until solid, then serve.

MATCHA BOOSTS METABOLISM AND BURNS CALORIES AS WELL AS WORKING TO CALM AND RELAX YOU.

MINT IS FANTASTIC FOR PROMOTING HEALTHY DIGESTION AND SOOTHING YOUR STOMACH. IT HELPS REDUCE INFLAMMATION IN THE BODY.

KALE – BERRY ICE CREAM

2 frozen bananas
240ml coconut milk
Handful of kale
4 dates, pitted
250g frozen blueberries
2 teaspoons vanilla extract
6 ice cubes

Serves 4

Not only is this a yummy, refreshing, healthy treat for adults, it's also a great way to get your kids to eat a dairy-free, sugar-free ice cream that even has a dark, green leafy veg inside it – which they can't see!

Combine all the ingredients in a blender or food processor and watch how quickly these ingredients morph into an incredible, nutrient-dense ice cream.

Pour into a freezerproof container with a lid and freeze for a couple of hours until solid.

Depending on your mood and what you have to hand, you could top a bowl of this ice cream with fresh fruit, chia seeds or bee pollen.

IF YOU'RE DETOXING, THEN **KALE** IS YOUR BEST FRIEND. IT'S FILLED WITH FIBRE AND SULPHUR, WHICH ARE BOTH GREAT FOR KEEPING YOUR LIVER HEALTHY.

FIG BARS

2 tablespoons chia seeds
6 tablespoons water
180g oat flour (or grind your
  own from rolled oats)
70g coconut palm sugar
1 teaspoon baking powder
½ teaspoon ground cinnamon
60g coconut oil, melted
1 teaspoon vanilla extract
4 tablespoons almond milk

For the fig filling
15 dried figs
2 tablespoons coconut palm
  sugar
Dash of water

baking tray lined with
  parchment paper

Makes 12–16

I adore figs and those moreish figgy biscuits you
can buy. But this is a much healthier twist on those
biscuits, which are filled with white flour, white
sugar, eggs and butter. I've opted for coconut palm
sugar, oat flour, and also use chia seeds in place
of eggs. I think you'll find these just as tasty, if not
more, than the shop-bought kind!

Soak the chia seeds in the 60ml water in a small bowl
for 10 minutes. Preheat the oven to 180°C/Gas 4.

Combine the oat flour, coconut palm sugar, baking
powder and cinnamon in a large mixing bowl.

Combine the soaked chia seeds, coconut oil, vanilla
extract and almond milk in a separate bowl.

Pour the wet mixture into the dry ingredients and
stir well, creating a ball. Place in the fridge for about
1 hour to firm up.

For the filling, put the figs, coconut palm sugar and
dash of water in a food processor and blitz to a paste.

On a floured surface, roll the dough out about 5mm
thick and into as much of a square as possible.
Spread the fig filling over half the dough and
carefully fold the other half over the filling. Cut into
12–16 squares, arrange on the prepared baking tray
and bake in the preheated oven for 12–15 minutes
until golden.

STUDIES HAVE SHOWN THAT EATING FIGS
INCREASES THE ANTIOXIDANT CAPACITY
WITHIN THE BODY FOR A SUSTAINED
PERIOD OF UP TO 4 HOURS.

BLACK BEAN BROWNIES WITH CHIA SEEDS

2 tablespoons chia seeds
6 tablespoons water, plus
  2 tablespoons extra, if needed
1 x 400g tin black beans,
  drained and rinsed
90g cacao powder
45g coconut oil, melted
1 teaspoon vanilla extract
1½ teaspoons baking powder
100g coconut palm sugar

23 x 30cm baking tin lightly
  greased with coconut oil

Makes 12

Black beans in chocolate brownies?! Absolutely! And they are incredibly easy to make, too – not to mention tasty and good for you. A 'no-guilt' brownie is one dessert recipe everyone wants in their repertoire.

Soak the chia seeds in the 6 tablespoons water in a small bowl for 10 minutes.

Preheat the oven to 180°C/Gas 4.

Put the black beans, soaked chia seeds, cacao powder, coconut oil, vanilla extract, baking powder and coconut palm sugar in a food processor and blitz together. If the dough appears a bit too thick, add a couple of tablespoons of water and mix again.

Evenly spread the dough into the prepared baking tin and bake in the preheated oven for 20–25 minutes. Remove from the oven and leave to cool before you cut into squares. They are meant to be gooey and melt in your mouth.

BLACK BEANS ARE PARTICULARLY HIGH IN FOLATE AND IRON – ESPECIALLY GREAT FOR PREGNANT WOMEN.

AVOCADO, CHOCOLATE AND LUCUMA MOUSSE

RAW CHOCOLATE MELTAWAYS WITH CHIA SEEDS

When you're running out of time but need a dinner-party dessert or something to whip up for the kids' pudding, then this is your go-to smash hit. Your guests will be shocked that this scrumptious dish is actually filled with fabulously healthy ingredients.

2 avocados, peeled, pitted
  and chopped
6 dates, pitted and roughly
  chopped
80g cacao powder
160ml coconut milk (or a
  plant-based milk of your choice)
1 teaspoon vanilla extract
1 tablespoon lucuma powder
Pinch of sea salt
Raspberries, to serve (optional)

Serves 4

Simply combine all the ingredients in a food processor and whizz to a creamy mousse. Scoop out into a serving bowl, chill in the fridge for at least 1 hour. Serve in lovely small bowls or cups topped with raspberries, if using.

If you're after a chocolate fix, look no further. The great thing about these meltaways is that they take just minutes to make and there's no baking involved. They are a wonderful, energy-sustaining snack.

20 dates, pitted
3 tablespoons raw
  cacao powder
1 teaspoon lucuma powder
2 tablespoons coconut
  oil, melted
1 teaspoon vanilla extract

To decorate
Chia seeds
Goji berries
Bee pollen

Makes 15 bite-sized balls

Put all the ingredients in a food processor. Blitz until well combined, then scoop into a bowl. Using your hands, mould the mixture into 15 balls, then roll each bowl in either chia seeds, goji berries or bee pollen to coat. Store in an airtight container in the fridge for up to 2 weeks.

LUCUMA IS A GREAT SWEETENER THAT IS LOW ON THE GLYCEMIC SCALE AND FULL OF NUTRIENTS, SUCH AS IRON, ZINC, BETA-CAROTENE AND CALCIUM.

CHIA SEEDS ARE A GREAT SOURCE OF OMEGA-3 FATTY ACIDS - THEY ACTUALLY HAVE MORE OMEGA 3 THAN SALMON!

KEY LIME PIE

90g rolled oats
45g ground flaxseed
40g hazelnuts
2–3 dates, pitted
2 tablespoons coconut oil,
  melted
2 tablespoons lime juice
Optional: For an even 'greener'
  Key lime pie, add 1 teaspoon
  spirulina powder while
  mixing the filling

For the filling
2 x 400ml tins coconut milk
2 avocados, peeled, pitted
  and chopped
Juice of 2 limes
3 tablespoons raw honey
45g coconut flakes

23cm pie dish greased with
  coconut oil

Serves 8

This is quite possibly one the greatest desserts ever. Whenever I see recipes for pies, I think I can't make them because they will take forever. But this recipe is totally different, as there is no baking involved. It's just a lot of good, wholesome ingredients mixed together over two layers to make a nourishing and eye-catching dessert!

Place the 2 tins of coconut milk in the fridge the night before you make the pie.

Combine the rolled oats, flaxseed, hazelnuts and dates in a food processor until finely chopped. Add the coconut oil and lime juice and pulse again until the mixture is combined. Press the mixture into the base of the prepared pie dish.

Wash the food processor ready to make the filling. Remove just the cream from the tins of coconut milk (save the water for a smoothie or soup) and blend with the avocados, lime juice, honey and coconut flakes until smooth. If you're using spirulina, add it now. Pour the filling over the base and freeze for 1 hour.

Serve right away or place in the fridge until needed.

LIMES MAY HELP PREVENT KIDNEY STONES, AS THEY CONTAIN MORE CITRIC ACID THAN ORANGES OR GRAPEFRUITS. CITRIC ACID IS A NATURAL INHIBITOR OF KIDNEY STONES.

PUMPKIN SEED, QUINOA AND OAT MUFFINS

6 tablespoons chia seeds
270ml water
180g oat flour (or grind your
  own from rolled oats)
70g wholewheat flour
1 tablespoon baking powder
1 teaspoon bicarbonate of soda
130g pumpkin seeds
370g cooked quinoa
480ml oat milk
60g coconut oil, melted
2 tablespoons raw honey
2 tablespoons coconut palm
  sugar

Muffin tray lined with 12 paper
  muffin cases

Makes 12

Sweet but wholesome snacks are a great way to satisfy cravings between or after meals and these oat muffins are just the trick. They are crammed with goodness and great to bring to a picnic.

Preheat the oven to 180°C/Gas 4.

Soak the chia seeds in the 270ml water for 10 minutes.

Combine the oat flour, wholewheat flour, baking powder, bicarbonate of soda and pumpkin seeds in a large mixing bowl and stir well. Add the cooked quinoa to the bowl.

Combine the oat milk, coconut oil, honey, coconut palm sugar and soaked chia seeds in another bowl and whisk together.

Pour the wet ingredients into the dry ingredients and stir well. Divide the batter between the paper muffin cases. Bake in the preheated oven for about 40 minutes, or until golden brown.

JUST A HANDFUL A DAY OF PUMPKIN SEEDS IS ALL YOU NEED TO GET 10G OF PROTEIN AND A SLEW OF MINERALS.

MINI CHEESECAKES WITH CASHEWS AND BLUEBERRIES

For the base
12 dates, pitted
50g almonds
90g ground flaxseed
1 teaspoon vanilla extract

For the filling
250g cashews, soaked
Juice of 1 lemon
60g coconut oil, melted
120ml raw honey
200ml coconut milk
150g blueberries

Cupcake tray lined with
   12 paper cupcake cases

Makes 12

Who doesn't love cheesecake? Baked or chilled, traditional or with a twist, there's something so tempting about this creamy dessert. But the ingredients! There's not much health there, unfortunately. So, here's a twist on an American staple that is now super-healthy and super-yummy. **(See photograph on pages 154–155.)**

Start by soaking your cashews in water for 3–4 hours.

Meanwhile, make the base. Put all the ingredients in a food processor and blitz to combine. Divide the base evenly between each of the cupcake cases, pressing down with your fingers.

Wash the food processor. After the cashews have been soaked, drain and rinse them and add them to the food processor with the lemon juice. Add the coconut oil, honey and coconut milk and process until smooth. Transfer the filling to a large mixing bowl and slowly stir in the blueberries. Spoon the filling over the crusts, cover with clingfilm and freeze for 3 hours.

Remove the mini cheesecakes from the freezer 1–2 hours before serving.

EACH OUNCE OF CASHEWS CONTAINS 21 PERCENT OF YOUR RDA OF MAGNESIUM. MAGNESIUM IS ONE OF THE MOST OVERLOOKED MINERALS. IT'S VITAL FOR MORE THAN 300 CHEMICAL REACTIONS IN THE BODY, INCLUDING ENERGY LEVELS AND RELAXATION.

HEALTHY CRISPY RICE BARS

180g almond butter
180ml brown rice syrup
2 tablespoons vanilla extract
150g puffed rice (or crispy rice
  cereal)

20cm square baking tin lined
  with parchment paper

Makes 12–16

These are another favourite of mine, but they are always made with sugary cereal and lots of butter and marshmallow. I wanted to come up with a much healthier alternative, not only for my kids to enjoy but for me, too. The result was so satisfying that I recommend taking a little square with you on the go for when you need a sweet pick-me-up.

Heat a large saucepan over a low heat and add the almond butter, brown rice syrup and vanilla extract. Stir well until thoroughly combined, then transfer to a large mixing bowl. Stir in the crispy rice until well coated and mixed.

Transfer the coated crispy rice to the prepared tin and press down to distribute evenly. Leave to set in the fridge for 10 minutes, then slice into squares or bars.

BROWN RICE SYRUP DOES RAISE YOUR
BLOOD SUGAR, BUT IT DOESN'T MAKE YOU
CRASH LIKE REFINED SUGAR DOES BECAUSE
IT'S A COMPLEX CARBOHYDRATE.

MANGO, BANANA AND BLUEBERRY ICE LOLLIES

2 bananas
2 mangoes, peeled, pitted
  and chopped
Handful of spinach
190g blueberries
360ml coconut milk
80g chia seeds

8 ice-lolly moulds (and sticks,
  if needed)

Makes 8 ice lollies

These are so pretty and can be made in a flash. They're great for those hot days when you need something refreshing that's also jam-packed with goodness. This goodness comes not only from the fruit, but also from the spinach and chia seeds that I've added… and no one will ever know!

Put all the ingredients in a blender or food processor and mix until smooth.

Pour the mixture into the ice-lolly moulds. If your moulds didn't come with sticks, push your sticks in, then freeze for 3–4 hours and enjoy!

MANGO MAY JUST BE THE KING OF FRUITS AS IT'S PACKED WITH LOADS OF ANTIOXIDANTS AND SUPER–HIGH IN VITAMINS C AND A.

INDEX

ACKNOWLEDGEMENTS

This whole thing had to start somewhere, right?! And the journey to here began with the start of my food blog and some very amateur photos! And so my beloved husband, Luke, must be acknowledged for not only taking over the camera and making the photos SO much better, but for his patience over the years with me and my 'crazy ideas'.

To John and Caroline Sandwich, my in-laws, for the unfaltering support, generosity and love they have shown to their very American daughter-in-law.

It's sometimes tough not having your real mother around (she lives in the US), so I also want to thank Susan Benn, whom I sometimes refer to as my surrogate mother. Maybe it's because we both came from the American Midwest that our bond began, but it continues to grow with each margarita and every hug telling me: 'You can do this!'

To Sarah Thompson, Briony Newman and Andrea Urquidi – my yoginis. Yoga means 'union' and united we are, not only in yoga but also in friendship.

And then there is the friend that's been there from the beginning. The one that's seen it all and – eight combined kids later – is still there. Thank you, Ruth Sturgeon, for being the best date on our 'date nights' together where four hours at Eight over Eight still isn't enough time to catch up.

And I'm not even sure this book would be here right now if I hadn't met you, Marissa Hermer, on the crazy rollercoaster ride we are currently on together. So thank you for the introduction to my wonderful agent, Charlotte Robertson, who in our first meeting together said 'yes – you've got something, let's go out and get it'… and we did. We found Céline and Jane at Quadrille who 'got it'. From that first meeting together, you both believed in me and for that I am forever grateful.

This book is everything I imagined it to be – it's exactly how I wanted it to look and for that I thank Nikki Ellis for the perfect design, Yuki Sugiura for the gorgeous photos and Iris Bromet for finding exactly the right props to style the food with.

This book begins with a dedication to my four children and so it seems only fitting to end it with them. Emma, Jack, William and Nestor – all I ever have to do is think about you and a smile is guaranteed to come across my face.